THE BIG
BOOK OF
BEER

THE BIG BE

Everything you Need to Know about

BOOK OF BEER

the World's Greatest Drink

CAMRA
BOOKS

ADRIAN TIERNEY-JONES

To Keith,
I think it's your round.

First published in 2005 by Campaign for Real Ale
230 Hatfield Road, St Albans, Hertfordshire AL1 4LW

www.camra.org.uk

© Campaign for Real Ale 2005

ISBN 1 85249 212 0

A CIP catalogue record for this book is available from the British Library

Printed and bound in Belgium by Proost

Head of Publications: Joanna Copestick
Editor: Carolyn Ryden
Editorial Assistance: Emma Lloyd
Marketing Manager: Georgina Rudman
Picture Research: Sarah Airey and Nadine Bazar
Design/typography: Dale Tomlinson
Typefaces: Kingfisher, Bliss & Shire Types (typography.net)

'BEER IS PROOF THAT
GOD LOVES US
AND WANTS US
TO BE HAPPY'

BENJAMIN FRANKLIN

CONTENTS

INTRODUCTION

This is a book about the best long drink in the world; the most refreshing drink in the world; the most companionable; the most versatile; the most thought-provoking…and if that isn't enough to drive you to drink, beer is also the bestselling long drink in the world.

As I reveal, beer has been around since Adam and Eve (even though Eve was probably a cider drinker given her record). The Ancient Egyptians loved nothing better than to polish off a pint (or whatever their measure was), while the equally ancient Sumerians lifted their beakers to a female god of beer called Ninkasi. Ancient Britons, Romans, Vikings, Lombardians, Flems, Tudor monarchs, monks, knights, preachers and politicians — all have enjoyed a glass/ram's horn/beaker of beer down the ages. This may come as a surprise given the way that global brewing corporations (and many smaller outfits), newspapers and assorted media, chefs, commentators and blinkered drinkers treat beer. Wine is revered while beer is seen as second best, a drink to be piled high and sold cheap.

Hold on a minute though? Do you fancy a beer? Look through the pages ahead of you and you'll learn about the beer styles of countries throughout the world. How about a cool and crisp best bitter served in a British pub steeped in the heart of its community? Or a spicy, quenching Belgium witbier, delivered to your table by a beer sommelier who actually knows what he is talking about. Or maybe you want to travel further. In these pages you'll find a rich and dark stout from Sri Lanka; a mind-numbingly strong stout from the state of Delaware; a spirited wood-aged ale from the cultured streets of Edinburgh; a smoked lager from the Franconian medieval town of Bamberg; a tart and quenching lambic from the mean streets of Brussels; a golden lager, bursting with floral notes, from the Czech Republic. The list goes on and on. Still fancy a beer? I thought so…

This book is also an attempt to prove that beer is the new wine. There are beers for instant refreshment, the Sauvignon Blancs of the beer world. There are beers for savoring and spending time with – the Merlots of the mash tun, the grand crus of grain. There are beers for every occasion: for sharing with friends and family, for serving with a simple lunchtime pizza or to accompany a sumptuous grand dinner, or simply to enjoy with a good book at bedtime. There are plenty of beers with all the complexity, character and polish of a fine wine, and after you've read this book I hope that you will know that asking for simply 'a pint of beer' is akin to going into a restaurant and asking for a plate of food, or going into a library and asking for a book.

My cellar (OK, cupboard) offers a beautiful sight: strong, noble beers going back over 10 years, all of them maturing and improving like fine vintage wines – Thomas Hardy's Ale, Fuller's Vintage Ale, Gale's Prize Old Ale, Rogue's Imperial Stout, Goose Island's Golden Monkey, Chimay Bleu. This is a magic cupboard with lots of magical bottles containing bewitching flavours and aromas. As I write I am sipping from a brandy balloon of Worldwide Stout, a stupendous dark beer of Herculean strength brewed in America. If that sounds too heavy (too Chateauneuf du Pape perhaps), how about a glass of the Riesling of the beer world: Bitter & Twisted from Harviestoun in Scotland? This is a perky, fruity, aromatic, thirst-quenching golden beer, replete with fresh tropical fruit aromas and a dry, slightly bitter finish. It's one of the new breed of light-coloured beers offering plenty of the fresh aromas and flavours with which British brewers are beguiling discerning drinkers (and winning plenty of awards while they're at it). Bitter, porter, golden ale and mild remain the mainstays of many a British brewer, but they're being joined by Cornish wheat beers, Devonian fruit beers, smoked beers from Shropshire and heather ales from the Highlands. Wine may have a few tunes but beer offers a complete songbook.

It has always been said of any impressive politician that he or she has a hinterland, something beyond the hurly-burly of politics. It's the same with beer, as I hope this book demonstrates. Beer has a culture, an etiquette that would rival that of Jane Austen's characters in *Pride and Prejudice*. What do you do in a British pub? What do you call beer waiters in Köln? What should you expect when drinking in an American brewpub? Read the book and you will find out. Enjoy beer, enjoy life – this is the underlying theme of this book. Stay healthy, take pleasure in the civilising matching of beer and food, explore the world through a glass, learn about the brewers' art and why he (and she) do it. You can even collect beer mats should you so wish.

I first drank beer when I was 15. Four of us sneaked into a hotel bar in North Wales and ordered halves of Greenall Whitley's bitter. I can't remember what it tasted like but it was undoubtedly an unimpressive introduction to the world of beer. Not long afterwards I became a schoolboy regular at a remarkably tolerant hotel bar where we tried Manns Brown (like drinking brown paper I remember), Stone's keg bitter, Strongbow and Wrexham Lager. Fortunately I soon came across real ale after leaving school and was particularly fond of Greene King IPA, Everard's Tiger and Ruddles County. I also discovered global beer classics such as Budvar, Jenlain, Chimay and Schneider Weisse in my 20s (I blush a little when I recall putting a slice of lemon on the lip of the glass of the last beer), though I had to wade through a lot of Schlitz and Colt 45 before I encountered the products of the US microbrewing scene — a trip to New England in 1996 uncovered a magnificent choice of hoppy beers which I have enjoyed ever since. Being a journalist it made perfect sense to start writing about beer, once I knew a bit more about it. I began with the small breweries of the West Country, where I live, and found many passionate brewers and lovers of beer, before branching out to write about pubs and brewers across the country. Writing about beer takes in history, drink, architecture, social changes, people, food, literature and much more. I heartily recommend it. There is a whole world of beer, beer-makers and beer culture out there all waiting for you to discover them. Which brings me to this book.

If you've enjoyed a pint of Adnams Broadside, or a glass of Fuller's London Pride, tingled at the aroma on an Oakham JHB or sat down and wept at the perfection that is Timothy Taylor's Landlord, then this book is for you. If you've ever licked your lips with anticipation for a glass of American IPA, with its scorching bitterness and cooling fruitiness, or scratched your head with bewilderment at the extreme beers emerging from the USA, then this book is for you. If you've ever been bewitched by the soft, flowery aromas and palate tingling glee of a great German Pils or Helles, or danced with delight at the spicy, herby zip and zest of a French bière de garde, then this book is designed for you. *The Big Book of Beer* is for every beer-lover, whether you've been drinking great beers all your life or are just feeling ready to embrace the quality, authenticity, innovation and quirkiness that is the mark of a great beer. Never has the world of beer been so exciting than it is now, and I hope that this book will take you to the heart of this excitement and make you thirsty. Very thirsty.

ADRIAN TIERNEY-JONES

BEER BEGINNINGS

First made from **BARLEY**
thousands of years ago,
beer has been a popular brew
throughout many civilisations.
Take a trip through time with

BEER BEGINNINGS
and discover how the world's
favourite drink is made.

THE ROOTS OF BEER

8000BC AND ALL THAT

It is 8000BC in the land we now call Iraq. History's first farmers have begun cultivating plants, particularly grains, and keeping animals. One of the grains grown is barley. In the next few centuries someone creates a drink out of fermented malted barley. One day this will be beer. By 4000BC there is evidence taken from pottery shards that beer had become a popular beverage. By the time the Hanging Gardens of Babylon had become the Ancient World's top tourist attraction, beer was the drink of choice and woe betide any high priestess caught nipping out for a swift one. Death by fire usually followed. No amount of pleas to the beer goddess Ninkasi could save the transgressor from a fiery doom. Later on, beer, or *hek*, was the tipple preferred by those labouring on the Pyramids for the Pharaohs in Ancient Egypt.

Meanwhile, the Phoenicians travelled along the coasts of Europe and traded grain and brewing know-how with the natives. When the wine-drinking Romans invaded England they were appalled by the beer, cider and mead that the locals were drinking. Further north, Angles, Saxons, Jutes and Vikings all retired to beer halls after a hard day's fighting to toast each other with horns brimful of ale. But don't imagine that what these roisterers drank would have been anything like beer today. Instead of hops, herbs such as rosewood, bog myrtle, yarrow and thyme were added to balance the sweetness of the malt.

Brewing in the Middle East came to a halt in the 8th century under the rise of Islam, but Europeans forged ahead with women brewsters or alewives leading the charge. Monks also took their turn before the mash tun. The Domesday Book records the monks of St Paul's

Cathedral, London, as brewing over 67,000 gallons of ale a year, using barley, wheat and oats. In Central Europe, medieval monastic orders are considered responsible for the development of the cold-fermentation process. They stored their beers in the cool of deep caves during the summer months when it was too hot to brew. Centuries later, this fermentation process would separate lager from ale fermentation.

Until the 1500s, the main drink of the British Isles was ale, a strong brew of malted barley flavoured with spices, aromatic herbs or even tree bark. Beer was regarded as foreign muck, a hopped beverage fit only for Flems and Germans. The first recorded instance of hopped beer arriving on English shores has been traced

Left: Beer has been the drink of choice for people throughout the ages.

In the Middle Ages, brewing ale was part of a monk's daily duty.

Below: Even though hops were once blamed for fomenting rebellion, revolution is the last thing on the mind for these Victorian hop-pickers.

in Kent. Within a hundred years this prejudice had changed and by the mid-1550s hopped beer was the dominant drink. Ale never reclaimed its place.

Porter was the first big beer of the industrial age, sweeping through the inns and hostelries of 18th-century England. The emerging United States of America also caught the porter bug with President George Washington being known as a keen imbiber. Over in Ireland in the early 1800s, the patriotic porter-brewing Guinness family weren't keen on the rate of tax that they paid on malt to the English and so chucked some untaxed, unmalted roast barley into the mash. This led to the birth of Irish dry stout.

The early years of the 19th century saw the emergence of India Pale Ale, first brewed in London to last the long journey to India. Meanwhile, 1842 saw the development of a cold-fermented golden beer in the Czech town of Plzen (Pilsen). Lager was born and the beer wars between ale and lager began. One of lager's earliest successes was in the United States, where German immigrants brought their brewing styles and beer tastes with them.

By the 1900s, bitter, mild and pale ale were the drinks of choice in British pubs. In the 1960s, lager began its relentless march through British bars while brewers tried to wean drinkers onto gassy, fizzy and cold keg beers. Cask ale fought back and inspired a generation of microbrewers, both in Britain and the United States. Now, there is a beer for every occasion with brewers across the globe rediscovering old styles, reinventing traditional beers, taking part in brewing innovations and pepping up old favourites. Cheers.

back to the early 1400s, with a shipment destined for Low Countries merchants working here. There are also records of English brewers occasionally dipping into the hop sack. But hops didn't have a very good press. In 1450, the presence of hops in beer was blamed for stirring up the peasant rebellion led by Jack Cade

Raw power

Back in the 18th century, when brewers wore wigs rather than lab coats, a popular treat for drinkers was cockerel ale – complete with the king of the farmyard, coxcomb and all. A century later, the white ales of south Devon hit the spot with locals even though pigeon droppings formed part of the mix. Today's brewers decline the use of farmyard creatures and the by-products of a life in the fields, but one thing they do have in common with the beer-makers of yesteryear is the use of the same basic raw materials.

WHAT MAKES A BEER

THE RAW MATERIALS

Brewed from malted barley, hops, liquor (water to the rest of us) and yeast, beer, just as much as cheese, milk or beef, is an agricultural product with deep roots in the countryside. A pint of beer starts life in a field of golden, swaying barley. After ripening, the barley is harvested and the grains are taken to a malt-house, or maltings, where the first step of their transformation into beer takes place.

MAGICAL MALT

In brewing lore, malted barley is known as the soul of beer. The skill of the maltsters is to kick-start germination in the grains. This produces tough guy enzymes eager to break down the starch within the grain into soluble malt sugars. Try chewing a pre-malted piece of barley and you could break a tooth – it's as tough as stone. But once malted, it is pliable and chewy in the mouth – and quite tasty (similar to the breakfast cereal 'Grape Nuts'). These malt

sugars are vital down the brewing line for yeast to snack on during fermentation, producing alcohol and carbon dioxide. Quite apart from this essential process, malted barley also produces flavour and aroma and gives beer its distinctive palate of colours.

Germination begins when the grains are steeped in water, after which they are spread out to dry. The grains are turned over up to four times a day to prevent the emerging rootlets from becoming entwined with each other. Only a handful of British maltings still use the traditional floor-malting method of production where the barley is turned regularly by hand. The rest either operate a process called pneumatic malting, where the barley sits a metre deep on a perforated floor with air blowing through, or is placed in large circular vessels with turner machines slowly rotating through the grains. Before the germinating grains can achieve their full self-regeneration, the maltster stops the process and the grain is kilned.

A visit to the malt store of St Austell Brewery uncovers the full variety of malts in use by this Cornish brewer: Maris Otter pale malt (regarded as the Rolls-Royce of barley), chocolate (so called because it can replicate the taste of chocolate),

Top right: Sacks of malt await the mash tun at St Austell Brewery.

Far left: Malt, hops, water = beer (with a little help from the yeast).

Left: The maltings, where barley's long journey to the glass begins.

Munich (or Cornish Gold), malted wheat, flaked barley, lager malt, cara malt, crystal malt, amber malt, dark crystal malt, crystal rye, malted oats, brown malt and roast barley. The darker malts have been roasted for deeper colour, body and flavour. Crystal malt is what gives a pint of bitter its gorgeously full-bodied flavour as well as its rich colour. It is made by a process similar to toffee-making. Next time you visit a brewery, taste some grains of crystal malt and the toffee connection is all too evident.

BEER PEOPLE

'My quest for the best barley'.

MIKE POWELL-EVANS, *head brewer at Adnams, Southwold, Suffolk*

Mike Powell-Evans (centre) checks the quality of the barley with grain merchant Cyril Adams and farmer Chris Lockhart.

'When I buy malt I am looking for high quality malt. I mainly buy Maris Otter barley and I can taste the difference between beers brewed with it and without it – there's a full biscuity flavour in the beers brewed with Maris Otter. It is important to visit the barley growers. Farming is on the edge and malting barley is a marginal crop. You need to talk to the guys on the farm to persuade them to keep growing. You need to keep in contact with them to know where they are going. I always specify malt grown in East Anglia and expect it to be malted locally. This saves on food miles, which is financially and environmentally friendly.

When I visit I am looking for a clean field with not too many weeds whose seeds could end up in the malt. It's also about having personal contact.

You have to have complete traceability so if Tesco's come to me with a bottle of Broadside I can go back to the field where the malt is grown. I will know which field the malted barley for that beer comes from.'

THE BREWING PROCESS

Once the malted barley is delivered to the brewers the fun really starts. After being ground the crushed malt, the grist, gets intimate with hot water in the mash tun for up to a couple of hours. When brewing British beers, pale ale malt makes up the main proportion of the mash with a dash of crystal malt for body and slight colour. Pale is the main malt used because it has the highest levels of starch and those enzymes which convert starch into fermentable sugars. A splash of malted wheat is often chucked in to help the beer retain its head when it is finally served. Dark malts produce tastes reminiscent of chocolate, fruit cake and espresso coffee, while roasted barley gives an Irish dry stout its distinctive burnt edge. During the mash the hot water prises the fermentable sugars away from the grist and what was a floury, crushed mixture of grain is left as a mass of empty husks after the potent liquid has been drained.

The run-off from the mash is called wort, a creamy Ovaltine-coloured liquid that also tastes a little like that venerable bedtime drink. The stronger the beer, the more malt is used in the mixture. To ensure that all the malt sugars are extracted during the mash, metal arms revolve above the mix spraying more hot water onto it. This is called sparging. The wort is now in the next stage of its odyssey towards becoming a beer. It is pumped into the kettle, or copper, and the boil starts.

LIQUID ASSETS

British brewers use water for cleaning their vessels and pipes, but 'liquor' is utilised for making their beer. Both are H_2O. Needless to say, a particular quality of liquor is essential for making good beer. Burton-on-Trent became a brewing centre because of the quality of its water and many brewers moved there. By the late 19th century brewers had learnt that they could add various salts to their liquor and so replicate Burton-on-Trent's famous liquor. This process is called Burtonisation and is continued by many brewers today – the main salts involved are gypsum (calcium sulphate) and Epsom salts (magnesium sulphate). Soft water is usually good for stouts and lagers (the soft waters of Plzen, for example, are just right for making Pilsner lager), whereas hard water, with its abundance of minerals, is good for bitter.

HOPPY TIMES ARE HERE AGAIN

If we were Taoists we would say that hops are the yin to malt's yang. Hops provide the fruity, bitter counterbalance to the biscuity sweetness of the malt. Just as yin and yang are supposedly the male and female principles locked in an eternal cosmic dance, so hops and malt get close and intimate throughout the brew and their balance governs the harmony of the beer. On a less metaphysical level, hops yield resins and oils from a sticky yellow powder called lupulin that is present in hop cones. These resins produce bitterness and have preservative qualities, while hop oils furnish flavour and aroma. Hence some hops are used for bitterness (kettle hops), while others are added later in the boil to provide their glorious aromas. On a more sensual side, hops give beer its zesty, fruity, spicy and carnal flavour. Hops eroticise beer. The mere whisper of names such as Pinot Noir, Cabernet Sauvignon, Grenache and Syrah have wine connoisseurs bowing down with religious fervour, but in the world of beer mention the words Goldings, Fuggles, Cascade and First Gold and ale-lovers will lick their lips in anticipation.

Hops come in the shape of dried cones or pellets and occasionally as hop oil, though aficionados frown on the use of the latter. They are added to the brew throughout a period of about 90 minutes – at the start, in the middle and right at the end. The first hops

Far left: Crushed malt and hot water get intimate in the mash tun at Hook Norton Brewery.

In the late 18th century, the Goldings hop was developed and 100 years later the Fuggles hop was introduced to the world. They became the two main hops for English bitter. The former gives off delicate lemony aromas and flavours; the latter has a well rounded, earthy bitterness and is used as a bittering hop.

thrown in are those picked for their bittering qualities while the ones at the middle and end are there to give that delicious and heady aroma that marks out a good hoppy beer. Sometimes the heat is switched off and the boiled wort is allowed to sit with hops steeping in the liquid for a while. Think of hops as condiments – the skill of the brewer is to add the right hops at the right time. Fresh (instead of dried) hops are occasionally used just after harvest to produce a spicy, fresh tasting beer in a process called 'green-hopping'. For a kitchen sink comparison, consider the difference between the use of fresh and dried herbs in cooking. One of the skills of the brewer is to pick the hops that will work together and then use the right quantities. In recent years there has also been a trend for single varietal hop beers that bring out the best from the hop used.

Left: Hop pickers get ready to Fuggle.

Below left: Hops provide the fruity, bitter counterbalance to the biscuity sweetness of the malt; below: St Austell head brewer Roger Ryman.

BEER PEOPLE

'Why I visit the people who produce my hops'.
ROGER RYMAN, *head brewer at St Austell, Cornwall*

'It is important to visit hop growers and pick the hops you will use for two reasons. First of all you need to look at the hops you are going to buy. Getting the right hop is the difference between a good beer and a great beer. The other important thing is having a good relationship with your hop grower and merchant.

September is the time when I visit. It's one of the nicest times of the year in brewing; it's the time when I really love being a brewer. Hop farms are in attractive rural areas such as Herefordshire and Worcestershire or further afield in Slovenia and the United States, which is where I get hops for our Tribute beer. Hop-growers are usually very nice people who are close to the soil and the earth. They live the agricultural year. People forget the agricultural origins of beer, that it is dependent on a year's harvest. There is all the talk about wine vintages but hops also vary from year to year.

I look at a series of samples from different fields and different growers. What I am looking for is a nice bright green colour, plus an absence of twigs, pests and disease. I take a sample, squeeze it and feel the moisture. Then finally I rub it between my hands for aroma – the most important aspect of all.'

BEER PEOPLE

'Do you know where your pint comes from?'

TEDDY MAUFE, *barley farmer, Norfolk*

North Norfolk farmer Teddy Maufe is at the forefront of a growing movement to educate drinkers about the connection between the barley he grows and what goes into a drinker's favourite pint. North Norfolk has always been noted for its barley which has a slower ripening due to the maritime climate. This produces excellent malt. During 2004 he opened a real ale shop on his farm and continues to try and raise the profile of East Anglian beer and barley.

'We are a 1,000-acre farm and 200 acres are given over to Maris Otter. A lot of our barley normally goes to Wolverhampton & Dudley but then we started becoming aware that we needed to do more locally and three years ago we started producing barley for Woodforde's. I met Brendan Moore at Iceni Brewery and talked about what could be done next. It all fitted into place when we went out to see our oldest son in San Francisco and drove through the Napa Valley. You could see lovely drives leading up to old houses, or what passes for old out there, and they were part of the vineyards. So here am I producing the grape equivalent in Maris Otter and I felt something similar to the California experience was called for. I opened the shop in June 2004, after two-and-a-half years work, and now it is up and running. There are 10 brewers represented, with 50 bottle-conditioned beers for sale. I want it to be like a vineyard so we can show how beer returns to its roots; we can show where the barley which makes it was grown.

There is also 100% traceability on the ales we sell here. We are so pleased with it all. People often think it's a mistake to have a shop out here in the middle of the country but when they come in and see pictures of barley in all its different stages on the wall they are usually pretty impressed. If you travel the wine regions of the world such as Bordeaux you are immediately aware of the enormous connection between the land and drink, but drive through North Norfolk and you wouldn't know what is special about the barley grown out here.

We grow the barley and it is floor-malted at Crisps in Norfolk and that's why we can offer full traceability.

One of the breweries we produce malt for, Fox, even put the grid reference of the field the barley came from on the back label of their beer bottles. We also wax lyrical about the sea fogs which come in and help the barley; we call them a "fret" down here. They extend the natural ripening process, which matures the barley and improves the quality even more. That's why coastal barley is so good. The soil is also good out here, light soil over chalk which is low in nitrogen and protein. We need to take the wine boys on at their own game.

We have lost the connection between the barley and the beer. Other countries are proud of their wines and beers, here we bumble along. For goodness sake it's Shakespeare's drink, the ale of England. I am passionate about it all, also proud about it, being Norfolk born and bred. This is a big tourist area and when tourists first come into the shop they look puzzled. They see the big avenue, fringed by trees and then they find the shop and I explain the connection. They say they never knew it – that there were so many brewers in Norfolk and that Norfolk barley was so good.

You go to a local town like Wells-next-the-Sea and the two biggest buildings there are old maltings. Go to other towns in the area and you will find blocks of flats called the Old Maltings, so the area was important because of the barley. I want to restore that connection.'

NATURAL ADDITIVES (OR NOT...)

Adjuncts are unmalted cereals such as torrefied barley (think popcorn in the back row of the cinema), maize, oats, rye, rice, sorghum or wheat, which are added to the mash tun in the first stage of brewing. They are there either to save money, to tweak the beer, or, in the case of rice, to help bring about a lighter colour. Sugar is also added to help with fermentation and colour. The German Purity Law permits only malted barley or wheat to be used as part of the grist. The Isle of Man has a similar declaration for its brewers.

The makers of the bestselling beer in the world are proud to include rice in the grist to produce a clean (although some would say bland) beer. Lovers of beer with flavour scoff, however there is a historical reason behind the use of rice in bestselling American beers. Brewers across the Atlantic, especially those located far away from the sea, have traditionally used six-row barley, which contains high amounts of protein and nitrogen that make a beer cloudy. Rice helps to dilute these amounts of protein and nitrogen. You could argue that because the use of rice and corn as adjuncts has been a tradition since the start of brewing in the United States, the likes of Anheuser-Busch are exceptionally traditional. On the other hand, you might agree with those who think rice is for curries, risotto and sake (essentially a rice beer).

Meanwhile, enterprising brewers have combined fruit, chocolate, liquorice, spices, herbs, coffee beans and honey with their beers (preferably not all at once). Some are gimmicks, while others are intriguing innovations or traditional styles brought up to date.

YEAST IS THE BEAST

After the boil, the hopped wort (as it is now known) is transferred through a cooling system before being pumped into fermenting vessels. The real fun starts as yeast is pitched into the cooled liquid and fermentation begins. This is where science gets its beer hat on. Before the action of yeast was explained by Louis Pasteur and others, it was a mystery named simply as 'goddisgoode' by brewers who turned to the Almighty when they couldn't work out how they ended up with such a potent brew. Yeast is a single cell fungus plant and a magical ingredient which

Right: Beer's long march to the glass continues with up to a week's slumber in fermenting vessels like these open ale ones at Hook Norton Brewery.

produces alcohol and carbon dioxide when it is added to the hopped wort prior to fermentation. It takes 34 million cells to produce just one pint of beer, so countless millions of these beasts get to work every time hopped wort is fermented. Without the use of yeast, the brewing process would leave us with a flat, horribly bitter, malty beverage lacking any alcohol.

In many small breweries dried yeast is used with a fresh batch for each brew ('pitch and ditch,' as one brewer calls it), while others prefer to skim the yeast off the top of a brew and save it for the next one. A yeast that has been used for the same beer over a period of time will have a specific character and adds its own particular imprint to the beer. It is believed that the vast majority of the 1,000 flavour components in beer are produced by yeast during fermentation. Different yeasts produce different flavours, so a beer brewed with a champagne yeast will taste significantly different to one made with bread yeast, ale yeast, lager yeast or even human yeast. If a brewer wants to create a beer stronger than 12%, he will use a yeast more suitable for champagne as ale yeasts tend to give up the ghost beyond 12%.

FERMENTING TIMES

The beer stays in the fermenting vessel for between four and seven days, depending on the brewery, and is then transferred into brewery conditioning tanks or casks (a process called racking). Finings are added to casks to clear the cloudy beer. Traditionally finings have been made from

Left: The rising, fluffy head of yeast is shown as beer ferments in open vessels at Tetley Brewery in Leeds.

Right: Proteins get hug-happy to form beer foam.

isinglass, once derived from the swim-bladder of the sturgeon. These days various species of threadfin, a member of the sturgeon family, are used.

Beers such as bitter are said to use top-fermenting yeast, where the yeast rises to the top of the fermenting beer and produces a large foamy head. Lagers are happy with bottom-fermenting yeast, where it sinks to the bottom of the fermenting vessel and works in a lower temperature than its ale cousin. However, these descriptions are too simple as the yeast has to work through the whole of the hopped wort to find and devour its malt sugars. Warm-fermenting (for ales) and cold-fermenting (for lagers) are more accurate descriptions.

Some breweries allow their beers to be fermented in open vessels and the glory of a rising, fluffy head of yeast is there for all to see (this is due to the relatively fast pace of warm fermentation). Others enclose their fermenting beer. Beer is usually fermented for up to seven days, though very strong beers can last longer.

Real ale emerges when the beer in the cask undergoes a secondary fermentation. Some brewers like to add hop pellets to their casks before they are sealed (once they used handfuls of whole hop flowers). This is called dry-hopping and gives a fresh hop aroma while slightly increasing the bitterness of the beer as it matures in the pub cellar. Next stop the bar-top and the pleasure of the pint.

> For very strong beers, a much longer boil takes place. Gale's Prize Old Ale has a three hour boil, while No 1 Barley Wine from White Shield Brewery in Burton-on-Trent gets a 12-hour boil in the copper, which evaporates ⅗ths of the volume and caramelises the wort.

FOAM SWEET FOAM

Nowadays, the presentation of beer is seen as all important by brewers, and if that includes a whipped-cream style of foam then that is what you get. Champions of foam insist that it makes a beer taste creamier and also looks good, while the residue of a lacy foamy pattern on the glass as the beer is drunk is also seen as a good thing. Many drinkers, though, think that the cult of foam has gone too far. CAMRA has campaigned for many years on the issue of a full pint, arguing that a heavy head of foam in a pint glass is a short measure. Lined beer glasses with room on top for foam have been created especially for this very job, though many in the industry aren't too enamoured with them.

What is foam? After the beer has been fermented and casked, proteins from the barley still remain. These proteins, along with other molecules, combine to hug each bubble of carbon dioxide in the beer, which is held together by polypeptide chains (with me so far?), thus creating a rock-solid, tightly held structure of bubbles – foam. The tighter the structure, the longer the foamy head will last as the glass is emptied. Simple isn't it?

How strong is your beer?

When you order a beer take a look at the handpump label. There is the beer's name and a number followed by % or the letters ABV. This is the standard scale of alcoholic strength, otherwise known as alcohol by volume – the percentage of alcohol in your finished beer. Most beers are between 4% and 5%, but back in the 19th century the average strength of British beers was around 5.5%. Alcoholic strengths started to fall as people demanded a beer that would both refresh and allow them to get up in the morning and operate machinery safely.

Nowadays, the age of the session beer is upon us, with the best prescription for a night out, or session, being bitters between 3.4% and 4.2%. Some drinkers feel that low-gravity beers have no taste but the presence of the delicious Brakspear's Bitter (3.4%) and the complex Hook Norton Best Bitter (3.4%) give short shrift to that particular myth. These days the challenge to all brewers is to produce a palatable low-gravity beer with plenty of hop and malt character without it being likened to water by the ever-critical drinker. Kaliber anyone?

Alternatively, there are plenty of beers with alcoholic muscle. These are blockbuster beers usually weighing in at well over the 8% mark. In the last few years, a handful of brewers have gone further and redefined the meaning of what constitutes a

strong beer. The Swiss (and now Austrian) lager Samichlaus was once considered the strongest beer in the world. At 14%, though, it was a mere stripling compared to what was to follow. Its record-breaking perch was taken over in the mid-1990s when Barry Parish at the Parish Brewery in Leicestershire brewed the humongous Baz's Super Brew – 23%. It was only made once and sold on draught or in bottle at the Old Brewery Inn where Parish was then based.

Inevitably American brewers have taken up the challenge to create their own super-strong beers. Sam Adams brought out a one-off 24.5% Millennium Beer. Those that have tasted it say it was more akin to a whisky than a beer. Then feisty micro Dogfish Head stunned drinkers with a Worldwide Stout of 21%. What a marvellous beer it was: dark black-brown with a loose cappuccino-coloured head; on the nose there was a powerful punch of coffee beans, chocolate, lots of malt and Christmas cake; the palate had more dark malts, chocolate, treacle, molasses and coffee, leading to a cherry brandy-style warming finish with plenty of hoppiness bringing up the rear. It was incredibly complex and didn't feel like a 21% beer. Since then travellers from the United States have come back like beery Marco Polos reporting sightings of 20% ABV fruit beers, Kaiser Lagers, Imperial IPAs, Double Milds and Quadruples.

> Government advice on alcohol is that men can drink up to 28 units a week and women up to 21 units. A pint of a session beer usually has a couple of units in it, but obviously the stronger the beer the more units it has.

BEER NATURALLY

ORGANIC BEER

If a drop of beer is good for you, think what wonders its organic cousin will work. Free from additives, pesticides and also kind to the countryside, no wonder drinkers with a conscience plump for a pint of organic ale. The seeds were sown with Golden Promise, launched by Edinburgh brewers Caledonian in the early 1990s. Other brewers took note and many now have at least one organic beer in their portfolio. There are even a handful of organic-only breweries, including the Organic Brewhouse on the Lizard Peninsula in Cornwall, Black Isle Brewery in the Scottish Highlands and the Marble Brewery in Manchester, who all boast that their beers are suitable for vegans. In mainland Europe, organic beers usually get the prefix bio. Examples include Wallonian brewers La Caracole, whose organic version of their wheat beer La Troublette is soft, honeyed and wine-like on the palate. Further north in Brussels, lambic specialists Cantillon produce an organic gueuze. Meanwhile, over the border in Germany, Munster brewery Pinkus Muller also looks to organic materials for its beers.

So what is so alluring about organic beer? Discerning consumers want the best ingredients these days, and organic is perceived as supreme, both in price and quality. Many drinkers also like to be environmentally friendly and organic materials are guaranteed free of pesticides and genetic modifications. According to Andy Hamer at the Organic Brewhouse, 'non-organic hops are sprayed 16 times in season, but with organic ones clover is grown in between the rows, which attracts the predators who go for the aphids on the hops. Non-organic barley is also sprayed as a matter of course.'

Then there's the foodie effect. A lot of discerning eaters and drinkers are exceedingly picky on flavour – think of the success of farmers' markets and the demand for exotic spices, herbs, vegetables and fruit. For beer, this has meant a surge in demand for those flavoured with herbs, spices and fruit as well as those using interesting hops from home and abroad. Organic beers are part of the same trend, even though few say that they can taste the difference. Finally, there's also something satisfyingly worthy about organics – by choosing an organic ale, you're saying that you care about the planet.

After all the hype, what does organic beer taste like? Are we being presented with wonderful organic beers which will knock spots off ordinary non-organic ones? Not necessarily. The secret of good beer is in the recipe. Environmental altruism has its limits when presented with a bad beer, even if it has been lovingly nurtured without recourse to pesticides. Many organic beers taste wonderful, the odd one does not. It comes down to the skill of the brewer as well as the raw ingredients. So it seems that organic beers are really a lifestyle choice, not a taste choice. You pay for what's NOT there (pesticides, etc). Some people, of course, beg to differ. Andy Hamer freely admits that he started the Organic Brewhouse for environmental reasons, but he also flies the flag for taste. 'Organic beers seem to taste differently from non-organic ones,' he says. 'They taste better and there seems to be a cleanness of flavour, and people who have drunk the bottled versions of my beers say that they have a fuller flavour.' And that's what good beer, organic or not, is all about: flavour.

TERROIR

Terroir is the term used to describe the effect of the local environment, history, farming practices and climate on the product. In the world of wine, the very concept of terroir adds value, prestige and romance to certain vintages. Winemakers can tell stories about steep south-facing slopes, granite soils, low rainfall and all-year sunlight which have oenophiles turning claret with excitement. Can beer be said to have a similar terroir? Most certainly. The ingredients of beer have a terroir, that magical attachment to place. Here's Kentish hop grower Tony Redsell on the effects of the local temperature on his hops: 'The exposure to the salt-laden north-easterly winds in March, as the character of the hop is being developed, gives an East Kent hop that unique aroma, which is just that little bit different from common or garden (yard) Goldings or Goldings types.' Taste and savour Shepherd Neame's Master Brew or Spitfire to experience this uniqueness.

For richer hop aromas we have to travel further west to Herefordshire and Worcestershire, where breweries such as Teme Valley, Hobsons and Wye Valley make use of the hops grown on their doorsteps. The rich clay soils in the area help to produce these lush hoppy scents. Here the Fuggle hop is king (though other hops are also grown). This is a magnificent bittering hop, which adds a sensuous earthiness to beer, but also contributes a tropical, grassy aroma.

In East Anglia, both large and small brewers use locally grown barley that is also malted in the region. Beers such as Adnams Best Bitter and St Peter's Suffolk Gold possess a richness and maturity in their malt flavours, which could be ascribed to the rich low-nitrogen soils of the region. Then there is the water of Burton, gypsum-rich and hard as iron, which was ideal for sparkling pale ales in the 19th century, making this Staffordshire town the centre of brewing. Until Burton's water could be replicated chemically, beers brewed in the town had an identity that could be ascribed to terroir.

Brewers might not be able to ascribe the qualities of their beers to the angle of the sun on the mash tun or whether it was raining when the fermentation took place, but the raw materials of our favourite beers all have a story waiting to be told, whether it's hardy hop bines struggling in the cold winds of East Kent during March and April, when the flavour and aroma of the hop begins to form, or sturdy stalks of grain taking their time to mature as another summer sea fog rolls in along the north Norfolk coast.

The ingredients of beer have a terroir, that magical attachment to place.

BEER FILE

From BITTER to **PORTER**,
BARLEY WINE to **STOUT**,
beer styles are as diverse and interesting
as any grape variety.
The BEER FILE provides everything
you need to know for creating a
discerning beer palate,
whether drinking in the pub,
at home or with food.

IDENTIFYING TYPES OF BEER

THE FOOLISHNESS OF ASSUMING THAT A BEER IS JUST A BEER

An American beer connoisseur goes into a restaurant and orders a glass of his favourite beverage. He is handed a standard, mass-produced lager and grimaces as he takes a sip. He then asks for the wine list. After studying it for a few moments he requests a bottle of Thunderbird, a wine long regarded as the street-person's choice of drink. The waiter looks aghast and replies, 'We don't do that sort of wine here sir'. 'Then why,' asks the diner, holding up his glass of fizz, 'do you do that sort of beer?'

This apocryphal story typifies the attitude of many restaurants and bars towards beer. Every effort is made to ensure that the wine list is as comprehensive as possible – there are Chardonnays from France, the United States and Australia; Pinot Noirs from Burgundy and Oregon, and Malbecs from the gaucho badlands of Argentina. But beer? Well, the prevailing attitude seems to be that it's just beer, isn't it? In the aftermath of the diplomatic kerfuffle that accompanied French President Jacques Chirac's dismissal of British cuisine in 2005, one celebrity chef weighed in with his thoughts. The said restaurateur had cooked for Chirac at Downing Street and was aghast that the president was downing beer with his food. But what sort of beer was it? Was it a full-bodied, malt-accented bitter from the Highlands and Islands which can sweep away all rivalries and sit down in comfort with the roast beef of Old England? Or was it spicily hopped golden ale from the downs of Dorset or the flatlands of the East Anglian Fens? Or maybe it was brawny barley wine that had matured for months in the cellar of a family brewery of ancient lineage, more than a match for the best cheese. Licensees and bartenders, sommeliers and even those who throw dinner parties and answer a guest's request for a beer with a querulous, 'I think I've got a can of lager somewhere' should all take note. Beer is more than beer: wine might have a few good tunes but beer has the entire orchestra.

How to taste beer

Beer-tasting should involve all the senses, even hearing – who doesn't love the satisfying hiss when a bottle top is taken off, heralding the promise of a well-conditioned beer? What's more, beer has a variety of aromas and tastes, all naturally produced by the actions of all the raw materials. Alchemy indeed.

The 10 Steps to Heaven

1   Look at the beer. It should be clear (unless it's a Bavarian Weisse or a Belgian witbier).

2   You can also judge a beer's condition by seeing how lively it is. A tired beer lacks sparkle and is dull in colour. When tasting the beer, this lack of life is all too apparent. Well-conditioned beer should dance, not flop, on the tongue.

3   As the beer descends down the glass, a lacework-like trace of foam should remain.

4   Swirl the beer around the glass to release its aromas.

5   Note the beer's colour, which varies according to the malt used; or in the case of stronger beers the consequences of a longer boil.

6   One of the great joys of a beer is its aroma. Is it malty, hoppy or fruity? Malty aromas include dried fruit, coffee beans, biscuit, smoke, malt, Ovaltine, plain chocolate, toffee, butterscotch and caramel. Some dark beers suggest rich Christmas cake. Malt also produces a dryness to the finish. Hoppy aromas are fruity, resiny, aromatic, citrusy, peppery, herbal, spicy, lemony and floral. It's possible to pick out Seville orange marmalade (sometimes even lime), tropical fruits such as lychees and passion fruit, resin (think varnish), blackcurrants and even fruit-flavoured candy. With some of the stronger beers the yeast esters add their own complexities such as tropical fruit, banana, apricot skin and a spritzy feel; strong beers sometimes also have a warming feel due to their high alcohol content.

7   Don't be afraid to stick your nose into the beer and spend time sniffing – even in a pub with friends. Try this for an experiment: hold your nose and sip your beer. You won't taste much as part of the flavour of beer comes from its aroma.

8   Taste the beer. Our tongues are delicate instruments which detect sweetness at the tip, salt and sour on the side and bitter at the back. Let the beer wash over your tongue and concentrate on the flavour sensations that you pick up. The rich palette of aromas mentioned above will be reproduced on the tongue to varying degrees of intensity. Some beers come bearing plenty of fruity flavours, while others boast rich, malty savours. What is the essence of the beer in your mouth? Is it smooth, tingling, grainy, thin, acidic or chewy? Some beers are robust on the palate while others slip down like honey.

9   Do swallow. Unlike wine-tasting, where you can spit all day long, part of beer-tasting involves letting the beer work its effect on your throat. In classic English bitters you will feel the dryness and bitterness. A great beer is well-balanced: the malt and hops work together rather than overwhelm each other.

10 Consider the beer's finish. Is it bitter? Is it dry? Does it last? Does a hint of malt return? Does it make you want another? It should.

MEET THE FAMILY

Beer is a family, with barley forming the DNA link. However, like all families, beer has many different members. The simplest division is between ale and lager, but that doesn't take into account the varieties that exist within these two camps. Here is a selection of the most common styles of beer, including a list of other beer styles across the world that demonstrates the global family of beer.

DARK

Once upon a time in the pre-industrial age, a lot of beer would have been dark.
As it was difficult to control heat during the kilning of malted barley in the maltings,
the grain all too often ended up charred, which affected the colour and taste.
Dark, when referring to the colour of beer, ranges from deep chestnut to opaque black
with a reddish blush at the edges. Think beers with history, or a sense of mystery.

Porter

According to legend, porter first emerged in the early years of 18th-century London and brewers all over the British Isles went into overdrive to satisfy the thirst for this dark and hoppy beverage. The name came from its popularity with London porters, who did most of the carrying and fetching in the capital. Fortunes were made and family dynasties founded – this was the age of the Whitbread and the Guinness families. Porter's long decline began in the Victorian age as the emergence of India Pale Ale and pale ale created a desire for lighter beers. Brewing was also big business and it was uneconomic to keep vast vats of maturing porter in deep slumber for months when lighter, fresher 'running beers' could be shipped out constantly to pubs. This decline continued across the 20th century until both American and then British microbrewers rode to the rescue. With today's revivalist porters expect plenty of malty and fruity flavours and aromas, as well as hints of coffee, chocolate and even condensed milk!

RECOMMENDED: Alaskan Smoked Porter (US); A Le Coq Porter (Estonia); Anchor Porter (US); Baltika Porter (Russia); Bateman's Salem's Porter; Burton Bridge Porter; Emerson's London Porter (New Zealand); Exmoor Beast; Fuller's London Porter; Okocim Porter (Poland); Porterhouse Plain (Ireland); Ringwood XXXX Porter; Rogue Mocha Porter (US); Sierra Nevada Porter (US); Stone Smoked Porter (US).

Stout

The strongest porters were called 'stout' porters. It was left to a canny Dubliner by the name of Arthur Guinness to develop the distinctive Irish dry stout style that would sweep the world and make his surname and stout virtually synonymous. Stout has now come out of the Guinness shadow with many breweries across the world producing their own versions, all boasting the characteristically roast and tangy bite of true stout. Imperial Russian, sweet 'milk' and oatmeal stouts are variations on this dark beer theme.

RECOMMENDED: Black Biddy (Ireland); Coopers Best Extra Stout (Australia); Dogfish Head Chicory Stout (US); Desnoes & Geddes Dragon Stout (Jamaica); Harvey's Imperial Russian Stout; Hook Norton Double Stout; Lion Dark Beer (Sri Lanka); Mackeson; Mitchell's Raven Stout (South Africa); Porterhouse Oyster Stout (Ireland); Rogue Shakespeare Stout (US); Titanic Stout; Tomos Watkin Merlin Stout; Wye Valley Dorothy Goodbody's Wholesome Stout.

STRONG

These beers are for sipping or serving with food, especially cheese or dessert; at the end of the day with a book on your lap or for impressing friends who think a dram is the only drink worth discussing; a winter's ale at the fireside or a nip in a glass to top off a night in the pub.

Barley wine

These richly endowed beers pleasantly please the nose with their smoky, fruity, nutty and toffee aromas, while they soothe the palate with warming alcohol, peppery hop, rich fruit cake and chocolate flavours. Some are light in colour, while others are dark and mysterious. American barley wine brewers up the hop ante, naturally. Plenty of malt goes into the mash tun to increase the alcohol produced by the yeast. Long boils to caramelise the malt sugars and extended periods of maturation are also common for this king of beers. The name is first glimpsed in the late 19th century when brewers perhaps wanted to bestow their beers with the same cachet as wine. Tap-room wags, however, christened barley wines as 'sitting down beers' because then there was far less of a distance to fall when you had supped a few.

RECOMMENDED: Adnams Tally Ho; Anchor Old Foghorn (US); Bush Ambrée (Belgium); Fuller's Golden Pride; Gale's Prize Old Ale; Robinson's Old Tom; Rogue Old Crustacean (US); Sierra Nevada Bigfoot (US); Woodforde's Norfolk Nips; Victory Old Horizontal (US); Young's Old Nick.

Vintage ale

Like fine wines, these bottled beers should be treated and laid down to mature and ripen over several years thanks to their immense alcohol and hop content. Those that are bottle-conditioned develop layer upon layer of flavour with the passage of time as the yeast continues to work. Thomas Hardy's Ale is the most famous example of the style and it was reputed to last 25 years, but at the start of the 21st century lovers of this beautiful beer were stunned when production stopped. Thankfully, Devon brewers O'Hanlon's took up the gauntlet and made a fantastic job of brewing it again. A good vintage ale will show different facets of its character for every year it's kept – providing you have the willpower! These are beers to win over wine buffs.

RECOMMENDED: Fuller's Vintage Ale; Lees Harvest Ale; Samuel Adams Triple Bock (US); Thomas Hardy's Ale.

India Pale Ale

India Pale Ales (IPAs) originated as heavily hopped dark-golden beers shipped to the British Raj in Victorian times. The high hop rate and alcoholic strength helped to preserve the beer on its long journey across swelling seas and through extremes of temperature. Burton-on-Trent's fame as a brewing centre really slipped into top gear during this period when it was discovered that the town's hard water and local breweries' unique methods of fermentation in union sets were ideal for IPAs. The name has been misappropriated by low-alcohol beers in the 20th century, but genuine IPAs are still produced by brewers with a sense of history and a love of hops. American IPAs are in a mouth-puckeringly high-hopped league of their own and brewers over the Atlantic are starting to produce Imperial IPAs with stunning amounts of hops and alcohol.

RECOMMENDED: Bridgeport India Pale Ale (US); Brooklyn Brewery East India Pale Ale (US); Burton Bridge Empire Ale; Darwin Brewery Rolling Hitch; Dogfish Head 90 Minute IPA (US); Downton Brewery Chimera IPA; Freeminer Trafalgar; Goose Island IPA (US); Marston's Old Empire; Meantime IPA; Pitfield's 1837; Sierra Nevada Pale Ale (US); Victory Hop Devil (US).

LIGHT

Light by name but not always light by nature. The eyes have it as a glass of golden ale, north German Pilsener or russet-hued best bitter sparkles on a summer's day. On the nose revel in the muscular bitterness and citrus twist of English hops, delicate aromas of orchard and hedgerow from fruit beers, or the heady scent of vanilla and cloves from a Bavarian Weisse.

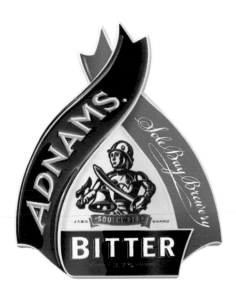

Bitter

The best British bitters are about a balance between biscuity, cereally maltiness and a citrusy and fruity hop character, with the bite of bitterness in the mix. They can be any colour from pale straw to deep russet. In strength they are usually around 3.5% for an ordinary bitter, 4% for a best bitter, while special or premium is stronger still. Bitter is naturally conditioned as it goes through a secondary fermentation in the cask in the pub cellar. Carbonation is low – bitter should be a gentle tingle on the tongue, rather than a frenetic dance of bubbles. These draught real ales remain the mainstay of British pub culture, where the call 'a pint of bitter' is a regular refrain. Pale Ales, such as Marston's Pedigree, are fruity close cousins, boasting a 'Burton Snatch' – a snappy sulphury hint on the nose thanks to the calcium sulphate in the Burton water. If brewed elsewhere this is replicated by Burtonisation, whereby particular salts are added to the brewing liquor.

RECOMMENDED: Adnams Best Bitter; Brakspear's Bitter; Coopers Original Pale Ale (Australia); Fuller's Chiswick; Hobson's Best Bitter; Goose Island Honkers Ale (US); Young's Bitter.

Mild

These are lightly or mildly hopped ales, known as four-ales before the First World War as they cost four old pennies for a quart. The title 'mild' is believed to have come from the habit of serving young and freshly brewed beer, rather than one that had spent some time maturing. It became popular with both agricultural and manual workers for its energy-giving, refreshing powers that were due to the richness of unfermented malt sugars still existent in the young beer. The new generation of milds are full of flavour and low in alcohol, except for a few where adventurous brewers have returned to mild's strong roots by upping the alcohol content. Most milds are dark in colour although a few contrary souls opt for a light mild. Ideal for a lunch-time pint or two.

RECOMMENDED: Bateman's Dark Mild; Coopers Dark Ale (Australia); Gale's Festival Mild; Moorhouse's Black Cat; Randall's Cynful; Sarah Hughes Ruby Mild; Teignworthy Martha's Mild; Victory Brewing Company Milltown Mild (US).

Fruit beer

Adding fruit to the brew is not a new idea. Kentish cherry ale was an old local favourite, while over the Channel in Belgium lambic brewers have been adding cherries to their beer for centuries, with the yeast on the fruit's skin helping to spark off a further fermentation. There are two main types of Belgian fruit-flavoured beers, one is the lambic flavoured with cherries (*kriek*) or raspberries (*frambozen* or *framboise*), while the other is a Flemish brown ale flavoured with cherries or raspberries. Brewers in the Low Countries also turn to lemons, blackberries, peaches, apricots and bananas for unusual flavours, though it has to be said that there's a hint of novelty to a banana beer. Elsewhere in the world, American brewers produce fruit-flavoured beers using whole fruit or syrups, while the old Melbourne Bros brewery in Stamford, Lincolnshire, is home to beers with cherry, strawberry or apricot flavours. Many other English brewers have got in on the act, though fruit extract flavourings are normally used instead of whole fruit. Whatever the mode of production, fruit beers possess fresh fruity aromas and flavours that entice new converts to the joys and complexities of beer.

RECOMMENDED: Belhaven Fruit Beer; La Choulette Framboise (France); Liefmans Kriek (Belgium); Meantime Raspberry Wheat Beer; Melbourne Bros Cherry; New Glarus Raspberry Tart (US); St Peter's Elderberry Fruit Beer.

Lager

Lager is the beer that conquered the world. From the Baltic to the Bahamas, from Australia to Iceland, if you ask for a beer you'll be handed a German or Czech lager facsimile going under the name of Pils, Pilsner, Pilsener or just plain lager. However, if you went into a bierkeller in Germany and asked for a lager, you'd be met with a puzzled look (though German bar-staff must have got used to Anglo-Saxon ignorance about their national beer by now). *Lager* in German means 'to store' and the long conditioning time of German beers is called 'lagering'. Over in Germany and Central Europe, lagered beers come in a variety of styles: Märzens, Bocks, Dunkels (dark lagers), Festbiers, Pilsners, Oktoberbiers, Helles, Budweis, Schwarzbier and Dortmunds. A real Pilsner or Helles is a wonderful beer with a fresh, spritzy and rounded palate of soft malt and a gentle hoppy, bitter finish, though the north German Jever Pils has an uncommonly ferocious bitter finish.

The fermentation process for lager differs from that of ale in that the yeast works in a much cooler temperature. It has always been called bottom-fermentation, though as the yeast works its way throughout the whole of the fermenting liquid it would be more correct to call it cold-fermentation. Once the first fermentation is completed, lager beers are put into conditioning vessels (or lagering tanks), where a full attenuation can take place over a few weeks, though a lot of cost-conscious companies have cut that time. Attenuation is a process whereby nearly all the malt sugars left are turned into carbon dioxide and alcohol, giving the lager a smooth, soft character. A few years ago, the very word lager would have been enough to send ale aficionados back behind their pints to utter curses against the fizzy, ice-cold amber nectar. However, even though lager still maintains its massive lead in the market, beer drinkers have learnt about the wonderful variety of authentic lagers in the past few years. For a start, eyes (and mouths) have been opened by the wider availability of traditional Czech Pilsners. American and British craft breweries have also started making real lagers that have bags of taste and character.

RECOMMENDED: Andechs Hell (Germany); Bitburger Premium Pils (Germany); Brooklyn Brewery Lager (US); Budweiser Budvar (Czech Republic); Cains Finest Lager; Jever Pils (Germany); Meantime Vienna Style Lager; Meantime Munich-style Festbier; Moortgat Bel Pils (Belgium); Pilsner Urquell (Czech Republic); Samuel Adams Boston Lager (US).

Golden ale

It is a mantra in the brewing industry that people drink with their eyes, and the last few years have seen the emergence of beers the colour of lager (or Chardonnay even), with fresh and fruity flavours to entice the unwary. These are cross-over beers, mainly produced by British brewers. As well as being popular with real-ale drinkers they have reached out to lager- and wine-lovers who are more likely to plump for a beer the colour of Chardonnay or Budweiser than a coal-black stout. On the nose expect lychees, passion fruit and pineapple aromatics all courtesy of the hop; on the palate, there is a clean and crisp flavour while the use of more modern hops such as tetang makes the beer zingy and moreish. Belgian golden ales are a different proposition in that they are stronger in alcohol with Moortgat's famous Duvel leading the pack with its fragrant aroma and dry, perfumy finish.

RECOMMENDED: Caledonian Deuchar's IPA; Crouch Vale Brewers Gold; Exmoor Gold; Harviestoun Bitter & Twisted; Hop Back Summer Lightning; Kelham Island Pale Rider; Moortgat Duvel (Belgium); Oakham JHB; Roosters Yankee.

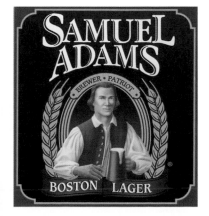

Wheat beers

Over 30 years ago, the wheat beers (*Weisse*) of Bavaria were dying on their feet. They were seen as an old folk's drink, rather in the way some people still view British mild. Then they became popular with hip young drinkers and eventually spread out from their Bavarian fastness to intrigue and inspire drinkers and brewers all over the world. At roughly the same time, Belgium's spicy *witbiers* (white beers) also appeared on the beer-drinkers' radar with Hoegaarden and its unique chunky glass leading the way. The re-emergence of these styles led British and American brewers to produce their own wheat beers, some of them influenced by the cloves-and-bananas character of Bavarian Weisse, others producing crisp, spicy and zesty ones in the manner of Belgian witbiers. A few brewers have struck out on their own and produced ale-tinged wheat beer styles. While cask beer is usually made with pale malt, plus handfuls of crystal or coloured malt to add subtle variations, wheat beers are a mixture of pale and wheat malt, with the latter making up a sizable percentage of the grist – this gives the beer a zesty, tart and refreshing flavour while subtle hopping gives a lemony, spritzy fruitiness. The colour of the beers ranges from pale gold to light amber. The Bavarian Weisse beers feature banana, clove and vanilla flavour notes (this is the work of the top-fermenting yeast) and are served cloudy (*hefe-weizen*) or clear (*kristall*). There are also dark wheat beers (*dunkel*) and stronger ones

called *Weizenbock*. Meanwhile the Belgium witbiers tend to be spicy and almost peppery, thanks to the use of spices such as coriander seeds and grains of paradise, as well as curaçao orange peel. There are also Berliner wheat beers, which have a tart and citrusy palate; they are traditionally served with a dash of fruit or herbal syrup.

RECOMMENDED: Du Bocq Blanche de Namur (Belgium); Gulpener Korenwolf (Holland); Hoegaarden (Belgium); Hopf Helle Weisse (Germany); White La Caracole Troublette (Belgium); O'Hanlon's Wheat Beer; Rogue Half-A-Weizen (US); St Austell's Clouded Yellow; Schneider Aventinus (Germany); Schneider Weisse (Germany); Schultheiss Berliner Weisse (Germany); Victory Whirlwind Witbier (US).

HEAVY

Heavy refers to mouth-feel with plenty of malty character and a full body. When a beer undergoes a long boil, some of the malt sugars from the wort are caramelised and stay behind during fermentation, giving a sweetish, rich and malty mouth-feel. These are cold climate beers with a low hop rate.

Winter warmers

Especially brewed for the winter months, these warming beers are well-rounded and fruity with a good balance of malty and hoppy flavours; there can be a slight sweetness in the finish. The use of various malts, especially crystal and chocolate malt, gives them a rich chestnut or mahogany colour. Some brewers add spices to the mix, which makes them particularly pudding-friendly. They are also known as Old Ales.

RECOMMENDED: Adnams Fisherman's Ale; Anchor Special Ale (US); Harviestoun Old Engine Oil; RCH Ale Mary; Woodforde's Norfolk Nog; Young's Winter Warmer.

Scottish ales

Traditional Scottish beers are dark and full of malt character with a slight sweetness. Hops weren't grown north of the English border so their use was carefully rationed; patriotic Scots brewers possibly saw hops as an English invention to be used as little as possible. A half of 'heavy' with a dram of whisky was a common tipple. Scottish or 'Scotch' Ales are stronger versions of this style, and particularly popular in Belgium where they have their own thistle-shaped glass.

RECOMMENDED: Atlas Three Sisters; Belhaven 80/-; Broughton Old Jock; Caledonian 80/-; Caledonian Flying Scotsman; Erie Brewing Company Railbender Ale (US); Orkney Dark Island; Silly Scotch (Belgium); Traquair Bear Ale.

MULLED ALE

Hidden away in the granary store of East Anglia, Norfolk brewers Woodforde's have been one of the most successful of breweries in the past few years. Their 4.6% winter ale Norfolk Nog is a beer to warm the cockles of the heart during the winter months, especially if used for the ancient practice of mulling, which was once common at the high table of Oxbridge colleges (mulled ales was also the main reason tankards once had lids, which kept the beer warm). The brewery's Managing Director Mike Betts explains: 'First of all find a traditional pub with a log fire. We put a poker in the fire and when it is hot put it into the glass of Norfolk Nog. The beer around the poker starts to boil giving it a vigorous white head. The aroma is fantastic and the head is warm with the beer beneath cool. Delicious.'

THE SHILLING SYSTEM

Scottish beers were traditionally called 60 shilling, 70 shilling or 90 shilling ales. The system still survives with Caledonian's 80/- and several other examples from Scottish breweries. However, it's very much a beer name that now belongs to the past, being a reference to the price of brewing barrels when things were measured in pounds, shillings and pence. It was first noted in the early years of the 19th century and was an indicator that the more expensive the beer, the stronger it was.

BEERS OF THE WORLD

A WORLD IN YOUR BEER

Beer is a global family, even if the loudest member of this tribe is the ubiquitous Pilsner lager style that straddles the world. Wherever you are, ask for a beer and you'll be handed a locally brewed version served as cold as the Arctic and with as much flavour as an iceberg. Stick to the original lager in the Czech Republic, or its close cousins found throughout the regions of Germany.

Despite the presence of the above relative, the world of beer is a family you won't want to avoid. How about visiting the likes of Sri Lankan porters, Japanese black beers, Alaskan smoked porters, American IPAs, Mexican Viennese red lagers, Belgian Scottish ales, rich and dark Polish Imperial stouts, German smoked beers and strong Bocks? Then, for something lighter, there are elegant Czech Pilsners, delicate Bavarian Helles, spicy Saisons from Wallonia, Kölsch, Alt, Märzen, Trappist, bière de garde (the French don't just think about wine) and, of course, the mad uncle of the family, lambic. All these should make the world of beer a lifetime obsession.

If you think beer is just beer consider this list of world beer styles and their variations

Stout: chocolate stout; coffee stout; cream stout; foreign export stout; Imperial Russian stout; Irish dry stout; milk stout

Porter: Baltic porter; brown porter; coffee porter; honey porter; Imperial Russian porter

Mild: imperial mild

Bitter: best; Extra Special Bitter (ESB); premium; strong

Brown ale: American brown ale, English brown ale; Flemish brown ale

India Pale Ale (IPA): American IPA, Double or Imperial IPA; English IPA,

Finnish Sahti

Pale ale: American pale ale; Australian pale ale; Belgian pale ale; English pale ale

Barley wine: American barley wine; English barley wine

Old ale

Vintage ale

Winter ale

Fruit beer: Flemish brown ales flavoured with fruit; fruit beers such as blackberry porter, apricot ale and banana bread beer; fruit lambics

Kölsch

Weisse bier: Bavarian; Berliner; north German

Witbier

Alt

Schwarzbier

Lager: American; Bock; Budweis; Doppel Bock; Czech black lager; Czech Pilsner; Dortmunder Export; Eisbock; Festbier; German Pilsener; Helles; Japanese rice lager; Maibock; Märzen; Rauchbier; Schwarzbier; Steinbier; Vienna Red

Arctic ale

Golden beer

Stock ale

Rye beer

Abbey beer

Trappist

Saison

Scottish

Lambic: lambic, fruit lambic, gueuze,

Red ale: Irish Red, Flanders Red

Bière de garde

Wood-aged beer

Summer ale

Speciality beer

Trappist beers

Six Belgian breweries are entitled to carry the appellation 'Trappist' and all are run by monks with brewing carried out on the premises (not always by the monks). There also used to be a single Dutch Trappist brewery but it lost the right to be called so when it farmed out its brewing to a secular company. The super six are Orval, Westvleteren, Westmalle, Chimay, Rochefort and newcomers Achel. These are rich, complex and very individual beers which should be served in stylish goblet-shaped glasses to help the drinker appreciate their wonderful aromas.

RECOMMENDED: Orval; Westmalle Tripel; Westvleteren Abt

Abbey ales

These are beers that were once brewed under the supervision of men of God, but at some time in the past have been leased out to commercial brewers to produce. It is estimated that at least 16 abbeys benefit commercially from this arrangement. Other beers boasting religious iconography are just marketing exercises. These beers are divided into two styles: the dark coloured Dubbel and the blondish Tripel, which is usually much stronger in terms of alcohol. Several American craft breweries have caught the Abbey habit too.

RECOMMENDED: Maredsous 8, Moinette Blonde; Silly La Divina; Val de Sambre Triple Blonde 8°; Victory Golden Monkey (US).

A Trappist monk at Abbaye de Notre-Dame de Saint-Rémy, Rochefort, Belgium.

German speciality beers

Even though a glass of golden Kölsch suggests the lager route of bottom- or cold-fermentation, Cologne's unique beer is actually a top-fermenting beer with plenty of fruity aromas more commonly found in an ale. The same goes for Alt, which is exclusive to neighbouring Dusseldorf, though

Alt styles are popular in craft breweries in Japan and America. This is also fermented like an ale and is amber/copper in colour, with plenty of maltiness on the nose and the palate. The name Alt is popularly supposed to relate to the fact that the beer was brewed the old (*Alt*) way, before the onset of golden lagers.

Back in Bavaria, or Franconia to be precise, it's not all Weisse and Helles. The town of Bamberg is home to Rauchbier, or smoke beer. Here, malt is kilned over beechwood fires to give the beer a smoky character. Despite the smokiness, these are very appealing dry and moreish beers that go well with robust and smoked foods.

The former industrial city of Dortmund is home to Dortmunder Export, a style of lager that is drier and slightly stronger than the average Pils or Helles. It is a golden beer made in response to a demand by industrial workers for a beer that could quench thirsts after long hours spent before the foundry. Sadly, it's a beer that is now harder to find than it used to be.

Finally, one of the rarest German beer styles is Gose, a wheat beer which is flavoured with a little salt and coriander. It can only be found in Leipzig and the nearby town of Goslar, from where the name of the beer originated.

RECOMMENDED: Früh Kölsch, Reissdorf Kölsch; Schüssel Alt; Uerige Alt; Aecht Schlenkerla Rauchbier, Christian Merz Spezial Rauchbier; Kronen Export; Gose Ohne Bedenken.

Helles, Märzen and Bock lagers

Helles is the Bavarian answer to Pilsner (see page 41), a fresh-tasting, golden beer with a soft maltiness. Märzen is darker and stronger with plenty of soft, sweet maltiness balanced by a tart and spicy hoppiness. This is the descendant of a beer originally brewed at the end of the brewing season in March to be tapped in September when brewing started again amidst the hurly-burly of beer festivals. Oktoberfest beers are golden, malty-sweet versions of Märzens; these are the beers downed by thousands at the world-famous Munich beer festival. Bocks are even stronger lagers (between 6–7%) with fragrant hoppy noses leading to plenty of dark malt flavours on the palate. They have their distant origins in the north German brewing town of Einbeck before the style was appropriated by Bavarian brewers, who also came up with Doppel Bocks, which are even stronger and greet the drinker with a distinctly smooth malt character.

RECOMMENDED: Aldersbacher Klosterhell, Andechs Helles Bock; Andechs Doppel Bock, Augustiner Lagerbier Hell, Paulaner Festbier; Paulaner Märzen; Paulaner Salvator Doppel Bock.

Lambic

A handful of Belgian breweries, mainly based around Brussels, produce this unique style of beer. Unmalted wheat makes up at least a third of the mash; stale hops are used for their keeping qualities and, once brewed, the beer is left open to be fermented by airborne yeasts before being stored to mature. Old and young lambics are blended to produce sparkling, champagne-like gueuze, while cherries or raspberries can be added to produce luscious fruit lambics, not to be confused with the krieks and framboises made with Flemish brown ales as the base. As for taste, think of the sharpness and acidity of traditional farmhouse ciders. You'll either love them or hate them, but they are worth trying.

RECOMMENDED: Boon Oude Geuze; Cantillon Gueuze 100% Lambic; Drie Fonteinen Oude Geuze; Mort Subite Gueuze.

Czech Pilsners

These are the kings of the golden-lager style and come from the country that drinks more beer than anywhere else – even the workers in the factories have non-alcoholic beers on tap for refreshment during the day. The Pilsner style has been so watered down throughout the world with the production of premium lagers that you have to go back to the likes of Pilsner Urquell and Žatec to remind yourself of the delights of this particular beer. Expect an aromatic hoppiness on the nose, with a soft malt on the palate followed by a quenching bitter finish.

RECOMMENDED: Budweiser Budvar; Pilsner Urquell.

American beers

Mention American beer and most people think of Budweiser: a cold and crisp lager, a brand to be seen with and usually swigged straight from the bottle. But there's more to American beer than this. If you're looking for something a little different, with masses of taste and brewed with enthusiasm and professionalism, check out the beers of America's microbreweries. At the last count, there were about 1,800 microbreweries, brewpubs and regional speciality breweries in the States. Inspired by the real ale explosion in Britain, North America is now home to a veritable army of brewers who often look to British, German and Belgian styles for their initial inspiration but give their brews a distinctive twist. Chilli beer anyone?

The great joy of American craft beers is the sheer experimental enthusiasm of the brewers. Fruit beers, IPAs, Scottish ales, wheat beers, pumpkin beers, real lagers and other Germanically inclined beers are just a few of the styles that can be found over the Atlantic. At the Great American Beer Festival there are over 60 categories of beer to be judged, including wheat beers, Bocks, Extra Special Ales (ESBs), Belgian Saisons, double IPAs, coffee beers and porters, oak- and barrel-aged beers, beers made with fruit and vegetables and traditional American style lagers. Anyone still want a Budweiser?

American IPA

Highly-hopped versions of the 19th-century British Empire favourite have been developed by Goose Island Brewery, Sierra Nevada, Stone, and Dogfish Head, with the measurement of hops, known as the International Bittering Unit (IBU), reaching far higher than the 40s and 50s that is normal for beers most drinkers regard as hoppy. American mass-produced beers usually have IBUs of between 8 and 22. Enthusiasm and lots of hops are the keywords here. Watch out for the double IPAs which have even more hops and alcohol.

RECOMMENDED: Bridgeport IPA; Dogfish Head 90 Minute IPA; Goose Island IPA; Sierra Nevada Pale Ale; Stone Ruination IPA; Victory Hop Devil.

American lager

Anheuser-Busch make a great noise about using rice in the mash for Budweiser Lager, but it's more fun to play find-the-hop in this light, inoffensive beer. On the other hand, the complex and multi-layered American lagers from the likes of Samuel Adams and Brooklyn Brewery have a closer affinity to those produced over the Atlantic in Central Europe, where rice is something you serve with the dumplings.

RECOMMENDED: Brooklyn Brewery Lager; Samuel Adams Boston Lager.

American porters

Guinness stopped brewing porter in the 1970s and it looked as if a beer style that had spanned three centuries was about to join the dodo. Thankfully, the American microbrewery revolution saved porter from extinction as brewers dipped into their bags of dark malt to produce beers brimming with mocha and chocolate aromas and flavours, while being unafraid to take porter a step further with Imperial porters, smoked porters and, now, wood-aged porters.

RECOMMENDED: Alaskan Smoked Porter; Rogue Mocha Porter; Stone Smoked Porter.

American Extreme Beers

Bigger, faster, better, stronger seems to be the mantra for many American craft brewers, especially those involved in the Extreme Beer Movement. In January 2005, the Extreme Beer Festival in Boston had 20% abv fruit beers, Bourbon barrel-aged barley wines and Imperial Russian stouts and lagers brewed with chillis. Strong stuff, but the joy of these beers is that they all taste like beers (just don't drink them in pints).

RECOMMENDED: Dogfish Head 120 Minute IPA; Samuel Adams Utopia.

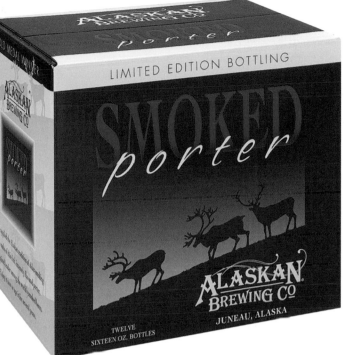

Taking it to the Extreme

Dogfish Head boss Sam Calagione on the brewing of Dogfish Head's Worldwide Stout, which weighs in at 21%, a prime example of an extreme beer which is extremely palatable.

'The brewing process is an adventure. We boil for about two hours and add some malt extract to the kettle to bump it up. We use a few different yeast strains to attack the wort. Primary fermentation takes almost two months and then the beer is aged for another month before it is bottled. We throw a lot of hops at it. But it is still on the sweeter side since there is a fair amount of unfermentable sugars. The taste profile is something like the biggest imperial stout you can imagine blended with a fine port. Most people who buy a case put six bottles in their refrigerator and the remainder in their wine cellar. The beer evolves and becomes more complex with time. It will improve for at least a decade.'

Australian pale ale

The land of ice-cold lager can seem a frustrating place for the beer lover in search of variety, but down in Adelaide, in South Australia, Coopers Sparkling Ale has befriended drinkers for years. It's a sparkling pale ale style that is bottle-conditioned and has plenty of fruity notes with a refreshing hoppy character. Coopers also produce other excellent beers, including a porter. Also to be recommended is Little Creatures brewery in Western Australia, who produce an eponymous Pale Ale which bursts with tropical fruit on the nose and a zinging hop-driven liveliness in the mouth.

RECOMMENDED: Coopers Sparkling Ale; Little Creatures Pale Ale.

Belgian Saisons

These are Wallonian beers whose history goes back to a time when brewing took place on farms and was seasonal. The difficulty of fermentation during the summer heat made sure that the mash tuns stayed silent leaving the farmers to get on with the harvest. Saisons are now brewed throughout the year, but are an endangered species. Expect spicy, hoppy flavours and aromas with a dry, herby finish. Very drinkable.

RECOMMENDED: Saison Dupont; Saison de Pipaix; Silly Saison.

Brasserie de Silly, Silly, Wallonia, Belgium

Silly by name but not by nature, the brewery is based in the middle of a bustling village north of Mons. The front of the building bears the name bold and proud. It's a frontage that implies beer, history, a pride in the product. It's a façade that also says comfort, says here we are in the middle of the community, from where their workforce comes. They are true local heroes. Brewing began in the area in the 1850s on what was then a farm – Saison beers have their origins in the agricultural community when brewing was a seasonal occupation.

The brewery was originally called Meynsbrughen, after the family name, but changed to Silly in 1970. Currently, the sixth generation of the family who started it all up remain involved. Didier Van der Haegen is the boss (his mother still bears the Meynsbrughen name) and an infectious ambassador for the brewery's beers that naturally include a Saison (5.3%). Other beers produced are a rich Scottish-style ale (8%), a fresh Pils (5%) and a complex Abbey beer called La Divina (9.5%).

Saison de Silly is a beer that was originally brewed for the family farm, then as other farms stopped brewing their own Saisons, Silly stepped into the breach. It is a blend of a matured and fresh beer with a vinous, earthy nose, reminiscent of an old Burgundy. It has a dry and lasting finish and a well-toned body that has obviously been going down the gym a lot. Drink it in one of Silly's several dozen bars dotted around the area (including one right next to the brewery) or take it home and serve with beef carbonade.

French Bière de Garde

The French might make a lot of noise about their wine, but beer is king in the northern part of the country bordering Belgium. The dominant style is *Bière de Garde*, which translates as beer to keep. Like Saisons, these mainly warm-fermenting beers have a history of being brewed in the spring so they will last the summer – hence their historical high strength of 6–8.5%. Now the brewing is a year-round process with the concept of bière de garde seemingly encompassing wheat beers and Tripel lookalikes. Presentation is important here; many of these beers are served in 750ml corked bottles not dissimilar to the champagne bottle (and it is this sense of style that makes them valuable companions on the dinner table). A gimmick? Not really. It has been pointed out by some writers that the region of Champagne is not that far away and farmers wanting bottles would have travelled there for their vessels. However, some early *Bière de Garde* producers were reputed to serve their customers with beer straight from the conditioning tanks. On the nose expect scents of spicy, herbal hop, chunky citrus aromas and an undertow of bready, warming maltiness, in some cases reminiscent of Bakewell Tarts. On the palate, a rich malty biscuitiness is accompanied by tangy citrus fruit and spirited alcoholic warmth. Many of the beers also boast a spicy almost herbal hoppiness, while some have the hint of an earthy, cellary character that adds plenty of muscle.

RECOMMENDED: Brasserie Annoeullin l'Angelus; Brasserie Bailleux Cuvée Des Jonquilles; Brasserie Duyck Jenlain.

Japanese Black Beer

Brewing has been carried out in Japan since the latter part of the 19th century, but until 1994 there was a dearth of small brewers due to a law that set the minimum amount of beer a brewery could produce to operate legally at a ridiculously high amount. This left the market to a cosy collaboration between four large brewing groups. With the repeal of this law, things have become more interesting and Japanese brewers, both large and small, occasionally tinker with beer styles producing wheat beers, sweet stouts and black lagers, which are dry, roasty and light-tasting versions of the German Schwarzbier style.

RECOMMENDED: Sapporo Yebisu Black Beer.

Czech dark lagers

Even though the lands of Bohemia and Moravia are best known for their classic golden Pilsners, dark lagers can also be found behind the bar. Some Czech dark lagers (close cousins to the German Schwarzbier) are low in alcohol and have a milk stout sweetness about them (they are meant for women apparently), while the stronger ones boast roasted malt and chocolatey noses with a rich and luscious palate. The most famous bar of all to uncover this unsung style of the land of Gambrinus is the ancient Prague brewpub of U Fleků, upon which beer lovers from all over the world converge to indulge in its luscious Flekovský Dark (4.5%).

RECOMMENDED: Herold Bohemian Black Lager; Kozel Premium; U Fleků Flekovský Dark.

Baltic porter

Over 200 years ago, British brewers found a market around the Baltic for their strong porters and stouts and, given that the Russian Empire owned most of the region, the beers were called Imperial Russian Porter/Stout. Catherine the Great was reputedly a great fan. One of the most noted makers of Baltic porter was a company in what is now Estonia set up by a Belgian businessman, Albert Le Coq, at the start of the 20th century. When the Bolsheviks seized power, the brewery was nationalized, but since the fall of the USSR it has become independent and their porter is brewed again (alongside a load of ordinary lagers and innocuous soft drinks). Sussex family brewers Harvey's make an Imperial Russian Stout based on the original records of the pre-Revolutionary A Le Coq brewery. Now you can celebrate the independence of the Baltic republics with these strong Baltic porters, descendants of the ones that travelled out there so long ago. Expect biscuity, roast malts on the nose, plenty of rich, cereally flavours, spicy hoppiness and a bitter finish.

RECOMMENDED: A Le Coq Porter (Estonia); Aldaris Porteris (Latvia).

BEERS FOR THE FUTURE

THE SHAPE OF THINGS TO COME

Back in the 1960s, those with a yen for predicting the future assumed that the 21st century would see us zipping around in our own helicopters while robots did the housework. How wrong they were. The brewing industry also fell victim to the same Wellsian dreams. Automatic beer dispensing machines were tried out while pubs entered the theme-bar age. On the beer-tasting front, keg was king and there were plans for fruit-flavoured beers. However, you could bet that the likes of giant industrial brewers Watneys and Whitbread (remember them?) would have plumped for Robinson's barley water rather than lambic as an inspiration.

Nearly half a century on, what about the future for beer? In the 1990s, one of the American brewing giants tried out a clear beer that they hoped would sell to women. It looked innocuous and tasted disgusting. On the other hand, the world of beer styles now encompasses a lot more than those swinging sippers of the Sixties could have predicted. Twenty years ago the thought of going into a pub and asking for a beer flavoured with honey, strawberry or heather would have seemed as likely as watching a recently released movie in your own front room. These days the likes of Fuller's and Young's have honey beers, while Bedford brewers Charles Wells has a luscious Banana Bread Beer and Badger's Dorset ales are infused with the flavour of peach or elderflower. In Liverpool Cains have had a big success with a raisin beer. Because of the success of these beers, especially at the dining table as well as with people who don't usually drink beer, expect breweries to continue experimenting with blends.

The other main influence on the future of beer are the innovations of the American microbreweries who have forged their own IPA style and resurrected the grand ideal of strong brown ales, stouts and porters. The Great American Beer Festival attracts a select elite of British brewers each year who are astounded by more than 60 categories of beer on display. At the extreme end of brewing in America look out for Imperial Kaiser Oktoberfest lagers, Belgian-style quadruples, double brown ales, wood-aged IPAs, 20%ABV fruit beers, double IPAs, double milds and beers made with most kitchen ingredients.

BEER GOES DOWN THE CHARDONNAY ROUTE

Maturing beer (or any alcoholic drink) in wood is not such a strange idea. Think of Chardonnay in oak barrels (or with a few toasted oak staves chucked into the cheaper blend), which is the king of the wine world. Critics of the practice think it takes the mystery and hard work out of producing a wine while its champions argue that it has brought full-bodied, easy drinking whites within the price range of those who won't, or can't, spend their hard-earned cash on big, buttery white Burgundies with a similar oakiness.

The idea of beer maturing in wood seemed to have gone out with the massive porter vats of the 19th century, while modern-day brewers had become loath to let their beers sit in the pub within a wooden cask, risking the chance of picking up off-flavours. Wadworth, Theakston and Samuel Smith still employ coopers for their barrels (Marston's also employs a team for maintaining their union sets), though finding their beer in the wood is getting harder and harder, despite the efforts of a pre-CAMRA organisation called the Society for the Preservation of Beer from the Wood.

St Austell in Cornwall has the St Kew Inn where the landlord lobbied hard and long to be able to sell his real ale in the old fashioned way, even though head brewer Roger Ryman has his doubts about such a method. The Ivy at Heddington, north of Devizes in Wiltshire, is another mecca for beer-from-the-wood fans. Here Wadworth's 6X and Henry's IPA can be tasted and enjoyed. As for the taste of beer from the wood, you need a divinely inspired palate to taste the difference, even though some claim that it settles down the sweetness of a beer. The appeal of wooden casks is aesthetic and they bring a hint of nostalgia to everyday drinking.

Elsewhere on the brewing front, we have Greene King's stupendous Strong Suffolk, which is a blend of a young fresh beer with the exceptionally strong 5X, a specially brewed beer that is kept for at least two years in oak. This two-year stay sees 5X absorb wonderful oaky flavours from the wooden vat as it reaches a strength of 12%. The resulting blend is much more controllable at 6%, but it remains a stunning dark, strong and fruity ale. Elsewhere, in Belgium, the sour red ales of West Flanders brewery Rodenbach undergo ageing in massive oak tuns, and deliver stunningly complex flavours and aromas. Meanwhile, across the Atlantic innovative and thrusting microbreweries have been maturing beer in wood for some time.

Alaska's Glacier Brewhouse puts a barley wine in Napa Valley wine barrels for one year, while their oatmeal stout spends six months within Jim Beam oak barrels. Dogfish Head's Detonator Dopple Bock is a strong lager that spends three months within oak wine barrels. The wood- and barrel-aged beers category at the Great American Beer Festival attracted 47 entries in 2004.

British brewers also seem to have been inspired by Innis & Gunn's Oak-Aged Beer (see p. 50–51), and American breweries' adventures. Cornish brewers St Austell have experimented by putting a bitter into a bourbon cask and a barley wine into a rum one. Meanwhile, East Anglian micros Elveden and Felstar and Welsh brewers Breconshire Brewery have also tried wood-ageing their beers. Knock on wood indeed.

Wooded vats at Greene King, where their strong 5X stays for two years before being blended with a weaker beer to make Strong Suffolk.

Innis & Gunn's Oak-Aged Beer

In the summer of 2003 Innis & Gunn's Oak-Aged Beer emerged and claimed to be the world's first oak-aged beer. Presented in a distinctive clear bottle and developed by Dougal Sharp, former head brewer at Caledonian Brewery in Edinburgh, this is a 6.6% beer which spends the first 30 days of its post-fermentation life resting in lightly toasted American white oak barrels. The big sleep continues for a further 47 days when all the barrels are emptied into a marrying tun and a further infusion and mellowing of flavour takes place.

The original idea for Innis & Gunn's Oak-Aged Beer came as family-owned distillers William Grant & Sons were buying beer from a Scottish brewer to assist in the production of Grant's Ale Cask Reserve Scotch Whisky. The beer was brewed to a special formula and used to flavour the whisky barrels, but no one knew what it would taste like when it had been in cask for a month. As soon as Dougal Sharp tried it he realised that it had potential and development started

'Oak-Aged Beer aims to provide the world market with a new style of beer,' said Dougal Sharp at the time. 'In the past beer was often stored in wood and there are still a handful of British brewers who keep that tradition alive. But we are, we believe, the first brewing company ever to use the fresh flavours of the imported 'first fill' oak barrel in this way to enhance the palate and complexity of the beer itself.'

When poured the liquid was a burnished gold with a hint of amber. On the nose there was vanilla, the buttery and oaky aromas associated with a Chardonnay or a good white Burgundy, cigar boxes and butter toffee. On the palate it was very full, with oaky, vanilla and butter toffee leading to a creamy finish with hints of whisky warmth, and a developing bitterness. It is an ideal dessert beer. Some have dismissed it as a novelty while others are more inclined to praise it as another branch of the beer family. Innis & Gunn even launched their own bespoke signature glass for the beer.

'This ageing builds in great complexity,' explains Dougal Sharp, 'and produces luxurious – yet delicate – flavours and aromas, which are just too good to leave trapped in the glass. We have therefore chosen glassware with a generous, open-mouth design so as to release the delicate vanilla, toffee, citrus notes for drinkers to savour.'

Innis & Gunn-man: Dougal Sharp.

BEER BREWING

Like *WINE*, **BEER** has a history.
Family brewers, long-established micros
and the latest brewpub,
all tell a story in BEER BREWING about
how their founders were seduced by one of
civilisation's oldest drinks.

WHO BREWS WHAT

A BRIEF HISTORY OF BREWERS

In the land of the Pharaohs, beer was so loved that its secrets were thought to have been handed down by the great god Osiris, which certainly made the brewers of the time popular people to have at a party. Millennia later, woe betide if the female brewers (or brewsters) of medieval England produced a bad ale. Carvings on the end of a bench in one old church depict an awesomely negligent brewster being led off to hell for her crimes against brewing. Nowadays, as the saying might go, he (or she) who brews bad beer gets no customers, but at least Satan is not involved.

The first brewers? Beer historians generally agree that Neolithic farmers in the Middle East (turn left at Babylon and head straight for Nineveh) kicked off the trend, making an intoxicating drink by baking a rough bread from barley, steeping it in hot water and then letting it ferment. Hardly hi-tech but it got them through the day. People settled, cities and towns were built, kings, priests and soldiers ruled the roost, and brewers made beer for them: one style for the upper class, and a rougher, less matured style for the rest. The division between the lounge and the public bar was born. In Ancient Egypt we find brewers making *hek*, which was produced on a scale large enough for one of the Pharaohs to hand out 10,000 hectolitres a year to the priests who ran the temples.

In northern Europe, after the decline of the Roman Empire, we find brewers plying their trade at the back of taverns or in the cloistered quietness of monasteries (it is estimated that there were up to 500 monasteries brewing beer in medieval Germany alone). No doubt home-brewing also went on in the odd hovel or three. A peck of barley and a handful of herbs and plants for flavouring (no hops then remember) and away you went. In medieval Britain, brewsters made ale as part of household duties.

As the Middle Ages came to an end, brewing entered its next stage. Brewsters and ale-house brewing were superseded by commercial brewers who organised themselves into guilds, got elected onto city councils and became members of the middle classes – one of the oldest still-functioning breweries in the world is home to Schneider Weisse in Kelheim, Germany. This was originally built in 1607, a few decades after English brewers started using hops. Nowadays, it is revered for its classic Bavarian wheat beer, Schneider Weisse, and its rich dark Weizenbock Aventinus. In the 18th century brewers in the British Isles made vast fortunes as massive vats of maturing porter covered acres in cities such as Bristol and London. The age of the beerocracy was about to dawn, as Messrs Guinness and Whitbread would no doubt have agreed.

The next century saw Burton-on-Trent become the centre of IPA brewing with a growing rail network enabling barrels of the beer to be sent across the country and then shipped around the world. Brewers from outside Burton (including Boddington's, Ind Coope and Charrington) built establishments in the town so that they too could brew Burton-style beers. It wasn't until the minerals in the local water were analysed that brewers realised that they could make their beers taste like Burton's by adding the relevant salts themselves.

Newly independent America also quenched its thirst with beer. After all, one of the first things the Pilgrim Fathers did on landfall was brew beer.

One of the oldest brewing companies still operating in the States is Yuengling, which began in 1829 – its home was declared a national historic site in 1976, and it is currently the fifth largest brewer in America. A few years later a Danish farmer called Christian Jacobsen opened up shop in Copenhagen, calling his business Carlsberg. Victorian Britain saw brewers snap up cheap public houses through which they could sell their 'running beers'. These were so called because, in comparison to the vatted porters that took months to mature, these beers were brewed, fermented, conditioned and drunk in the pub in a matter of weeks. The names of family and regional brewers such as Bateman, Adnams and Hook Norton were first mentioned by drinkers at this time.

Prohibition in the United States after the First World War destroyed a lot of the vibrant brewing communities and, when the Volstead Act was repealed by Roosevelt in 1933, some of the breweries that survived found themselves at the mercy of larger competitors. The age of corporate brewing, when accountants rather than the head brewer decided what went into the mash tun, was just around the corner.

The brewpub tradition was also on the wane in postwar Britain, with only four left by the start of the 1970s. By now, breweries across the world were merging, closing competitors and diversifying into hotel chains, restaurants, and other forms of hospitality and leisure. Brewing good beer was probably viewed as a troublesome nuisance. Family-owned breweries who resisted the siren call of money found themselves ploughing a lonely furrow, until the CAMRA-inspired defence of 'real ales' brought them new business. Even more importantly, CAMRA helped to kick off the microbrewery revolution, which started in Britain, then spread over to America, Canada, and throughout the world.

Nowadays, semiotics enter the fray with some brewers preferring to call themselves micros, which usually means a one-man-and-his-mash-tun operation or a brewpub, where a landlord (in Britain) or a brewery (elsewhere) sell their beer to a captive audience. Others prefer craft brewer, which involves a larger staff, and possibly some pubs to sell beers through plus a longer history. Whatever the title, these are all homes to good beer.

Now, small brewers across North America, Great Britain and, increasingly, in parts of Europe are combining enthusiasm, passion and skill to make beer, while long-established regional breweries, especially in the UK, seek out new markets for their great beers. All is not rosy in the beer garden, but thousands of years after the first brew was supped, beer is still here.

The Carlsberg Brewery in Copenhagen where Christian Jacobsen started brewing.

CRAFT BREWERS

THE BIRTH OF THE MICRO

The American and British microbreweries of the 1980s have grown up. Many celebrate 21 or even 25 years before the mash tun; others are in their second decade and have seen demand for their hand-crafted beers grow from year to year. Some have swapped owners, beers have changed over time, breweries have moved, and pubs may have been bought and sold, but the enthusiasm and passion that gave birth to the idea remain. Craft brewers are grown-up microbreweries. It's not just the English speaking world that has seen the revitalisation of brewing, as countries such as Germany, Belgium, France and Italy play host to new breweries set up by a variety of home-brewers, professional brewers and beer-lovers all eager to produce their own beers. In most of these countries this is a continuation of a venerable tradition – breweries were common in the small towns of Bavaria as well as in cities such as Köln and Dusseldorf, while the likes of Brasserie La Caracole and Val de Sambre fly the flag in Belgium for the small is beautiful movement.

Dent Brewery, *Dent, Cumbria*

Dent was set up in 1990 in a picture-postcard part of what is locally called the Yorkshire Dales, though it is actually in Cumbria. The founder was Martin Stafford, who quit corporate life in London during the late 1980s for a less stressful life as the owner of The Sun inn in the village of Dent. The brewery is sited in a converted stone barn where brewer Paul Goodyear was installed.

Acclaim for the brewery's beers started arriving in the late 1990s, when their rich and strong stout T'Owd Tup (6%) was voted Champion Winter Beer of Great Britain, while their full-bodied and fruity golden beer Kamikaze (5%) also won awards at the Great British Beer Festival. Other beers to savour are the session bitter Aviator (4%) and the warming 4.5% best bitter Ramsbottom (in an area like this it makes sense to look at matters ovine for naming the beers). Dent is one of the most isolated breweries in the country, but it's also in the midst of handsome scenery with the brewery tap, The Sun, apparently one of the most photographed pubs around. Interestingly, Martin Stafford's brother, Nick, also entered the brewing business with Hambleton Ales.

Hobsons Brewery, *Cleobury Mortimer, near Kidderminster, Worcestershire*

Hobsons was established by Nick Davies and his father in 1993 and sells its beers throughout Worcestershire, Shropshire and Herefordshire. These are local beers that rarely travel outside their area, a principle they feel very strongly about, though their bottle-conditioned beers can be found further afield. This policy of keeping it local has obviously worked as the history of Hobsons has been one of steady expansion; they are now a 20-barrel outfit. The beers they produce are classic English bitters made from hops grown eight miles down the road in one of the great hop-growing areas in the world. Its bestselling beer is the scrumptious Best Bitter and rightly so. This is a classic 3.8% session beer whose biscuity malt character dives into a stupendous charge of citrusy and fruity hops leaving behind a bitter and slightly dry finish. Other beers brewed include a nutty mild (3.2%), the sprightly golden ale Town Crier (4.5%) and the gentlemanly winter special Old Henry (5.2%).

Right: Clearing out the mash tun at Hobson's Brewery.

Kelham Island Brewery, *Sheffield, South Yorkshire*

'Don't give up the day job' is a commonly heard piece of advice. In 1981 college lecturer Dave Wickett took note and carried on with his students while taking on the Fat Cat in Sheffield, a classic Victorian pub where real ales from both regional and microbreweries were sold. In a city dominated by the products of four big breweries, this was an island of independent and intriguing ales. It soon started winning itself fistfuls of awards. In 1990, Dave went further when he opened a small brewery at the back of the pub. By 1999, this tiny little building was the biggest brewery in Sheffield as all the others had closed. Wickett always says that if someone had told him that this small room, now crammed full of brewery memorabilia, was going to be the biggest brewery in Sheffield by 1999, he would have said they were mad. The lecturer also went against the grain and chucked in the day job.

The risks paid off in the summer of 2004, when Kelham Island won Champion Beer at the Great British Beer Festival. This was for Pale Rider (5.2%), a strong and winsomely pale bitter that was partly designed for people who didn't want too much bitterness but liked strength and flavour. As the colour and name suggest, this is a golden beer with tons of fruit on the nose, passion fruit, grapefruit and biscuity malt on the palate and a dry finish with another helping of fruit salad. For a small craft brewer, winning Champion Beer of Great Britain brings its own problems. Everyone with a pub-license to their name wants a piece of the action and it can be hard to keep up with demand. Dave Wickett found a novel way to deal with the dilemma, by getting Essex family brewers Ridley's also to brew Pale Rider (under the name of Pale Island) to exactly the same recipe as the original with Kelham Island keeping a close eye on matters. Sadly Ridley's closed in 2005 and at the time of writing Wickett was looking to link up in a similar deal with another brewery.

Kelham Island Brewery has now moved to a purpose-built brewhouse yards from the Fat Cat, all of which stands in a former industrial part of Sheffield where street names such as Cotton Mill Walk recall the past. Redevelopment in the area is now imminent with luxury flats and a recreational park planned, all of which should bring more drinkers for Kelham Island's distinctive ales. Also try their Best Bitter (3.8%), a fantastically assertive bitter with plenty of biscuity maltiness, deep booming Fuggles hop notes and a classic Goldings citrus twist.

Mauldons Brewery, *Sudbury, Suffolk*

Mauldons moved into their new home at the start of 2005, an imposing-looking glass-fronted building situated high on a hill overlooking the market town of Sudbury. Behind the glass can be seen a gleaming collection of brewing vessels in a light and airy space. This is brewing at its most modern, with more than a hint of the American microbrewery culture, whose practitioners make a statement of their intention to brew. Mauldons has been running since 1982, with current owners Steve and Alison Sims buying it off the founder in 2000. The investment in this stunning new kit is obviously a sign of the Sims' commitment to brewing in a region whose history is so tied up with the making of beer. The sight of long closed maltings, now converted to other uses, is common in the small towns of Suffolk. The beers of Mauldons also demonstrate that close regional connection, boasting a rich maltiness that comes from local barley. Black Adder (5.3%), a potent bittersweet stout, has a dangerous drinkability, while for those seeking something less dark and chewy, the soft maltiness of strong bitter, Suffolk Pride (4.8%), is balanced by a gorgeously fruity hoppiness.

BREWERY PROFILE

The Brakspear Story

Brakspear Brewing Company, Witney, Oxfordshire

If beer is to have a relationship with its local environment, then the story of Brakspear acts as a cheerleader. The closure of Brakspear's Henley home in 2002 was greeted with groans of dismay from beer aficionados. However the property developers had their way and the site was redeveloped. The issue wasn't that the beer would no longer be brewed but that it wouldn't be brewed in Oxfordshire. Those intensely hoppy Brakspear beers were to be brewed miles from their Thames Valley heartland at Burtonwood in Warrington, and Oxfordshire had lost yet another of its best-loved local ales (Morrells in Oxford had gone towards the end of the 1990s). It wasn't just about flavour (although many insisted they could taste the difference between the beer when brewed up north to that brewed down south), it was also a case of local pride. During the beer's northern exile, several licensees reported that their locals were switching to other beers. Drinks wholesaler Refresh UK, who bought the brand, announced that they would be looking for a replacement site in Oxfordshire. Cynics felt sure that this was a smokescreen thrown to hide the unpalatable fact that Brakspear's beers were doomed to be another anonymous brand brewed at any old place. However, refreshingly, Refresh UK, led by Rupert Thompson, kept their promise. 'Brakspear's is one of the classic beers of England,' says Thompson. 'Brakspear's was definitely an Oxfordshire beer and so to move it out of the county wasn't right as people cared about the brand.'

In 2004, Brakspear's beers returned home to Oxfordshire, to be brewed at the Wychwood Brewery in Witney, ironically the town where Robert Brakspear kept an inn in the 18th century. Not only did the brewing return to Oxfordshire but the brewers also retained their famous 'double drop' system, in which fermenting hopped wort is dropped to a lower vessel during fermentation. This helps to rouse and aerate the beer and also to remove dead yeast and used hops. This system, along with the Maris Otter malt, Goldings and Fuggles hops and the unique and complex Brakspear yeast, all help to replicate the richness and flavour of the original beers. The return of Brakspear is a story of perseverance and faith. At a time when some in the brewing industry think that the local origins of beer are not important, the dedication of Thompson and head brewer Jeremy Moss and his team is both a surprise and a delight.

Brakspear Bitter (3.4%)

Light ruby/amber in colour; on the nose rich malt and spicy, peppery hop aromas dominate; on the palate grainy, biscuity malt hits the palate first before a citric orange peel fruitiness makes its appearance; there is bitterness and dryness in the finish. This is a wonderful beer full of character which tastes far stronger than it actually is.

Wye Valley Brewery, *Stoke Lacy, Herefordshire*
First set up in 1985 in the village of Canon Pyon, Wye Valley has spent time in Hereford before moving out to its current home in 2002. Two pubs are owned, including its former brewpub home Barrels, which no self-respecting lover of real beer visiting Hereford should miss. According to John Gardener from the brewery, 'The success of our beers is down to quality and sourcing good raw ingredients. For instance, all our hops are local.' Even though Wye Valley's beers are wholesaled throughout the country and can even be found in bottles in the United States, the brewery is very much in favour of celebrating its home county. Not only are the hops local, but the brewery also produces regular monthly specials that celebrate Herefordshire's history and wild life, famous locals and even a beer for both St David and St George – now that's what you call diplomacy.

Brasserie La Caracole, *Falmignoul, Belgium*
La Caracole started its brewing history in 1990 in the Wallonian capital of Namur, but several years later it moved out to the nearby village of Falmignoul and set up shop in an old brewery which had been active for nearly 200 years until its closure in 1971. This is a characterful home with lots of exposed brickwork, pallets, crates and logs stacked all over the place. One area has a bar where the brewery's beers are served, while the brewing equipment is to the front. Hold on a minute. Logs? La Caracole is the last brewery in Belgium to use a wood fire to heat up its boil, according to co-owner François Tonglet, who runs the place with Charles Debras. 'The reason we do it,' says this former home-brewer and beer-shop owner, 'is that it far more convenient and also more ecological

as it is easy to find wood to burn.' Five regular beers are produced, including a sumptuous and wonderfully refreshing witbier, Troublette (5.5%). According to Tonglet the aim was to get somewhere between a witbier and a gueuze. There are also plans for a fruit flavoured version. Dried peel from both orange and lemon are used in the mix, giving it a refreshing if understated tanginess, while the nose has both banana and clove notes. It's a unique witbier which provides essential refreshment on a hot day while also making good company with that great Wallonian delicacy of marinated fish, Escavèche. The other beers produced here are Troublette Bio, a winelike organic version of the witbier; a rich blonde of a triple Saxo (7.5%); the warming Caracole Caramel (8%) and a soothsayer of an ale called Nostradamous, which at 9.5% is full of deep, booming notes of chocolate, Mars Bars and cocoa powder, all balanced by resiny hoppiness and ending with a fiery alcoholic finish.

Brasserie Val de Sambre, *Gozée, Belgium*
Dangerously drinkable is the only description one can give to the Triple Blonde (8%) produced by the Brasserie Val de Sambre, a relatively new microbrewery which was set up in 2000 in the shadow of the ruined Abbaye d'Aulne, after which most of its beers are named. There's a creamy head with a complex nose of barley, orange peel, spices and hints of cumin, while it bathes the palate with a wonderfully tangy citrus character. Served in an earthenware goblet in the surroundings of a high-ceilinged bar next to the brewery, this is heaven on earth. Outside, it's not so bad either. This is a beautiful part of the world, a wooded hidden valley dominated by the Gothic ruins of the abbey, which met its nemesis during the years of the French Revolution. Back inside the brewery filled with cylindrical-shaped vessels, brewer Frederick Collinet crafts a memorable selection of ales named after the Abbaye d'Aulne (they used to be produced by Affligem until Val de Sambre set up shop in 2000). These are spicy, tangy, mouth-filling beers with the likes of coriander seed, powdered ginger, aniseed, cumin, grains of paradise and orange peel added in varying quantities. Try the Triple Brown (8%) or, if you're in the area before Christmas, make a bee-line for Abbaye d'Aulne Super Noël (9%), a rich, dark seasonal ale which is brewer Frederick's favourite.

BREWERY PROFILE

Moorhouse's Brewery, Burnley, Lancashire

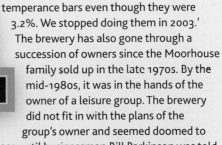

In the last few years, the Lancashire town of Burnley has hit the headlines for all the wrong reasons – there have been riots and the extremist views of some of the locals have been in the spotlight. However, 2004 saw the town receive a piece of better news. This was when Pride of Pendle, the fruity best bitter of local brewery Moorhouse's, was announced Champion Cask-Conditioned Beer at the brewing industry's Oscars – the Brewing Industry International Awards. Now, the brewery could call their 4.1% bitter the best cask ale in the world, which would join their Black Cat in the company's hall of fame – this luscious and creamy mild was voted the Champion Beer of Great Britain in 2000. The celebrations for the brewery continued in 2005 when Moorhouse's celebrated its 140th year. Not bad for a company which was known throughout most of the last century for its low-alcohol hop bitters. 'From 1930 until 1975 we only produced hop bitters,' says Managing Director David Grant. 'They went into all sorts of

temperance bars even though they were 3.2%. We stopped doing them in 2003.' The brewery has also gone through a succession of owners since the Moorhouse family sold up in the late 1970s. By the mid-1980s, it was in the hands of the owner of a leisure group. The brewery did not fit in with the plans of the group's owner and seemed doomed to close until businessman Bill Parkinson was told of the impending demise while supping a pint of Pendle Witch (a name inspired by the local area's dark history of witchcraft). He liked the beer so much that he brought the company and remains chairman today.

Across the road from the brewery, which can produce 50 barrels (or 1,800 gallons) in one go, is the General Scarlett, one of the brewery's handful of pubs. Named after a long-forgotten military hero of the days of Queen Victoria, this is the brewery's tap. If you can't get the beer right here then you won't get it right anywhere. Originally a betting shop, it's a traditional northern pub offering the brewery's splendid range of beers, including Black Cat (3.4%), Premier Bitter (3.7%), Pride of Pendle (4.1%) and Pendle Witches Brew (5.1%). Inside, it's welcoming and snug. Beer bottles and other knick-knacks range round the wall, joined by framed copies of Moorhouse's many winning certificates from the Brewing Industry International Brewing Awards and CAMRA. There is a stuffed fox's head on the wall above the entrance. In true northern style, the pub also offers pie-and-peas suppers. Local lad Peter Gouldsborough is the head brewer, having joined the company when he was laid off from his previous job as a carpet-fitter. 'We brew as we have always done in the last 20-odd years,' he says, 'and use only the best ingredients such as Maris Otter and the whole leaf hops Fuggles and Willamette, which are used in various blends. There is no need to use other hops; our products are not broke so why change them?'

Moorhouse's David Grant outside the award-winning brewery.

BREWERY PROFILE

Marcello Davanzo
Felstar Brewery

Marcello Davanzo, who is known to all and sundry as Franco, runs microbrewery Felstar in the wilds of North Essex near the village of Felsted; he is also a dedicated winemaker.

'I have been a real ale enthusiast for a number of years and always wanted to brew but had never taken it further because of different commitments. For instance, I also own the Felsted Vineyard which is the oldest commercial vineyard in East Anglia. I started to brew in January 2001. It was time to do some replanting, which is when you will not have a crop for four years or so, so I thought it would be a good idea to use one of the outbuildings to start a brewery.

I use the old bonded store of the vineyard for the brewery and I am still learning as I go along. I don't profess to be an expert brewer but sometimes that can be to your advantage: once you realise the limitations and the possibilities, you are more keen to experiment with different types of fermentation, different types of decoction and so forth. I have built the brewery to suit my needs. It looks complicated for what is a small five-barrel brewery, but allows me to do different types of beer from real lager to real ale. It is very much a hobby, a challenge and a passion. On the other hand it's no good doing it unless you can sell it. I am enthusiastic about

beer and am always searching for the holy grail of the perfect pint.

When I wanted to brew a honey beer I learnt about bees before making the beer. I joined a club, went on a course and now have the bees here at the vineyard. I am building a few more hives for the spring. I enjoy it, it's a lovely activity. Bees are very clever things. It's also nice to have your own honey from your own hives. I like the self-sufficiency of it. We were at the Chelmsford beer festival and someone said he wouldn't be surprised if I grew my own trees to make my own hives. I like to make the hives, do the bees. I also do some medieval styles of beer as well, I do one which is called Mild Knight made with nettles and wild hops.'

BREWERY PROFILE

Sara Barton
Brewster's Brewing Co.

Sara Barton of Brewster's brews on a 10-barrel operation in the village of Stathern near Melton Mowbray, Leicestershire.

'I have been brewing with my own brewery for almost seven years but brewed for Courage for three years beforehand. After my first degree in biochemistry I decided I wanted to continue my studies and I saw information about the brewing masters at Heriot-Watt University and thought it sounded really interesting and a way to apply the science I had learnt.

I started off brewing beers that I liked, not bitter astringent ones, but ones where you wanted another, with a good balance of malt and hops. I like a bit of hop in my beer but not overhopped, in the way some beers in the south are served, so in a way it's more of a regional thing.

It's a very sociable business and we all talk to each other regularly. People are prepared to share information and help each other more than in other industries I have experienced. I also enjoy especially on the micro side being able to develop new recipes and getting feedback from drinkers and what they do and do not like to drink.

The biggest grumble I have is the tied nature of the pub-trade where many publicans are not allowed to buy beer that their customers would like but have to choose from a very limited big brewer's list. Seeing our first brew being drunk in the local pub gave me a real sense of pride that people were enjoying what we had made. Winning the Country Living Rural Businesswoman of the Year 2000 was also acknowledgement from outside the industry that we had done well, while seeing our bottled beer on the shelves of our local Asda is pretty exciting as well.'

BREWERY PROFILE

Alastair Hook
Meantime Brewery

Alastair Hook, one of the most dedicated and exciting brewers in Britain. His Greenwich-based Meantime Brewery is home to a variety of handsomely crafted beers, including a London Porter, an IPA and several lagers.

'It all started for me when I was 16 and became a real ale fan. I used to go on trips to places like the West Midlands and Manchester and enjoy the local beers. A few of us then got into home-brew. When I went to Europe I was amazed by Belgian and German beers, especially the latter which were wonderful compared to British lagers. I went up to York University but was aware that I wanted to do something tangible with my life. Up in York I drank beers such as Sean Franklin's from Roosters and they were an epiphany. I thought 'this is what I want to do'. I was even more motivated when my stepmother said I should do something with wine which made me want to do the opposite.

By then I had also started working in the US during the summer and noted how cool the beer scene was over there. I travelled to a lot of micros and started getting obsessed with the flavour and taste of beer. I decided to do a brewing degree at Heriot-Watt University in Edinburgh, where I went for four years. The brewing degree was a bit of a let-down as the department seemed to have a 'stack it high, sell it cheap' approach. There wasn't even a society for brewing students so I went to CAMRA for a loan and we organised a beer festival and after that we started a society and visited breweries.

The degree was theoretical and very industry related. Beer for me was pure passion; it was also about quality and choice. It seemed that the only place where beer was understood was south Germany so I decided to learn German and went to the University of Munich for a post-graduate course in brewing. Suddenly I was doing what I wanted to do. Later on I went to work for Spaten and Kaltenberg but I missed London and came back in 1989 and worked for a brewpub in Ashford which was brewing German-style lager. It had a lovely copper clad, Bavarian-made double decoction kit, but it hit the wall and I realised that in the UK you are up against ersatz continental lagers.

In 1993 I was a co-founder of Freedom Brewery who made real lagers and was starting to meet people like Mark Dorber (see p. 91), and going to the States to judge at the Great American Beer Festival. After Freedom I went to Mash where I had complete freedom. I came up with a blackcurrant porter, for instance, which made complete sense to me. A porter is bitter-sweet as is a blackcurrant. The great thing about Mash is that all the staff were into the whole concept, whether it was wine, cheese, bread or beer. However I needed to do things myself and so I raised the money for Meantime. I felt that my visions for producing beer were more imaginative and cosmopolitan then most coming out of the industry – I felt more in tune with people like Sean Franklin and small SIBA members who were full of passion for making beer but had a frustration with distribution.

Frustration for me is that the industry pigeonholes things. Beer is diverse and there's no reason that beer shouldn't be regarded as well as wine. The 'Taste the Difference' range with Sainsbury has given me freedom, while our Grand Union pub has helped to educate people about beer. Good beer is all about flavour. When I was young I read a book that pointed out how beer has been the thread woven through British society. Beer was part of our society and culture once. What I love about beer is it's a social gel. It's fun. It's a mixture of romanticism and hedonism and passion for taste.

Choice is the reason I do such a large selection of beers. Think about the Bruce Springsteen song where he says that there are 500 channels and nothing on. You can go into an average bar and there are 50 beer- related choices but there's little choice in flavour. People like what they like if they get choice – I want to give people choice. Also give them a great time. We are entertainers; we oil the gearbox of society. We do mainstream beers from Europe, while my chocolate or coffee beers are the way-out ones. In the future we have double IPAs, a proper London Porter and an Imperial Russian stout being made. We brew with passion. People deserve choice.'

FAMILY BREWERS

KEEPING IT IN THE FAMILY

Family breweries have a history. Many are found in traditionally built Victorian breweries where beer has been made for decades. Others have moved from their old homes but still maintain their beery high standards. It was in the Victorian age when maltsters, farmers, industrialists and others with capital and a yen for a new business idea set up the family business. That is why the likes of Young's, Adnams, Fuller's, Coopers in Australia, Moortgat in Belgium and Schneider in Germany have members of the family in charge and can point to great-great-great-great grandfather as the man who started it all. Family breweries are also called regional, which refers to their local power base.

Adnams Brewery, *Southwold, Suffolk*
'Oh we do like to be beside the seaside', especially if there's a chance of a good local pint. This is exactly what visitors will find at the small east-coast resort of Southwold, where Adnams Brewery resides in the centre of the community. On brewing days a rich aroma of malt rolls over the town accompanied by the sight of a plume of white steam as the brewing coppers seek to supply the never-ending demand for the great beers of Adnams. But the pumping heart of Adnams is found at the brewery. Here the gregarious Mike Powell-Evans is the head brewer. His passion is such that he explains the mysteries of brewing in the clearest and most precise way, so that anyone who gets their mash tun mixed up with their copper goes away totally illuminated.

Adnams' beers have been beloved of real ale fans for decades. Once upon a time travellers had to brave the small railways and buses of eastern Suffolk to hunt down the likes of Broadside (4.7%) and Bitter (3.7%). However, in the last 15 years, in common with a lot of other regional beers which rarely emerged from their heartland, they have crashed out of Suffolk to beguile and bedazzle new generations of ale lovers, even if the best place to try them still remains its heartland around Southwold. Adnams Bitter is one of the great English bitters. Dark gold in colour it has a powerful biscuity, malty aroma with a citrus oranges-and-lemons fragrance hovering in the background. On the palate there's rich biscuity maltiness, elegant fruitiness with hints of orange before a muscular bitterness leads into a long, dry finish. Perfect.

Bateman Brewery,
Wainfleet All Saints, Lincolnshire
The wide expanses of the south Lincolnshire fens are only broken by the sight of church towers calling all good people to prayer, but when you disembark from the train at the small stop of Wainfleet All Saints the first thing you'll probably see will be a building celebrating John Barleycorn rather than the Almighty. A couple of hundred yards away from the station, the old redbrick windmill stands as a symbol of the enduring appeal of Bateman's, one of the best loved of family breweries. However, the story could have been so different with Bateman's becoming just another fondly remembered brewery, as back in the 1980s it nearly went under during a bitter family feud. The hard work of George and the late Pat Bateman saved the day and drinkers can still enjoy classics such as Dark Mild (3%), XB (3.7%), XXXB (4.8%) and Salem's

Bateman's Brewery: a symbol of the enduring appeal of this well-loved family brewery.

Porter (4.7%), while George's children Jaclyn and Stewart have both taken up the reins, so the future is assured. Family continuity is all important in breweries such as Bateman's.

There is a delightful and satisfyingly traditional feel to the brewery with its excellent museum featuring a range of old Bateman's artefacts, a massive bottled beer collection and a visitor centre where the beers can be enjoyed in pristine condition. Tours are regular and the scintillating aroma of the mash tun will sharpen anyone's appetite for a pint or two afterwards. The mild is a classic example of this much underrated style with its smooth, creamy mouth-feel, a grainy maltiness and subtle hop on the finish, while the bitters XB and XXXB both include Goldings hops in the mix to bestow a great combination of aroma and flavour. The brewery also produces a variety of seasonal beers, including Combined Harvest (4.4%), a unique ale with wheat, oats and rye joining the malted barley in the mash. As a result it's astoundingly complex with a rich citrus and toasty malt nose, followed by a slightly sweet and malty start to the palate with fruity bubblegum flavours joining in the fun. The bitter and dry finish is bolstered by lingering fruit and hop flavours.

Caledonian Brewing Company,
Edinburgh, Scotland

The capital of Scotland was once known as a city of beer, books and bibles. It even gained the insalubrious nickname of 'Auld Reekie', thanks to the number of breweries that drenched its air with the smell of 'the boil'. In the 21st century, Edinburgh's sole surviving brewery is Caledonian, which has been making beer since 1987, so this is a regional brewery by virtue of its size of production. Situated in a Victorian brewhouse, gas-fired open coppers give the hopped wort a vigorous rolling boil, which head brewer Robert Burton claims makes the brewery's beers, especially their main award-winning brand Deuchars IPA (3.8%), so unique.

Caledonian's beers have broken away from the dead weight of tradition. The Scottish beer drinker was reputed to love 'heavy', a beer that was best known for its sweeter, more malty character. Caledonian's bestseller throughout the 1990s was 80/- (4.1%), their gloriously malty take on this style. However, the king of 'Cally' ales these days is Deuchars IPA, which was feted as CAMRA's Champion Beer of Great Britain in 2002. This is a tremendously moreish beer with an initially soft and silky maltiness which is well balanced by a great attack of quenching citrus fruit; the finish is long and gently bitter. This is closer to a golden ale than any previous traditional Scottish beer, and thanks to the drive and quality control of the team at Caledonian. Deuchars IPA has become to Edinburgh what Guinness is to Dublin.

Back in 2004, Caledonian caused a bit of a stir among beer-lovers when it was sold to Scottish & Newcastle, though the management immediately bought back all the UK brand rights for the Caledonian beers, the right to brew by their own methods and recipes to all the beers. 'We manage the brewery for Scottish & Newcastle,' said Managing Director Stephen Crawley at the time, 'we now have one simple goal – we want to sell more Cally beer to the right outlets.' Time will tell whether Caledonian have made the right decision to join themselves to a multinational company whose corporate vision has, at times, seemed decidedly short-sighted.

Fuller's, *Chiswick, London*

When a man is tired of London, he is tired of life. In the past 50 years Doctor Johnson's much-repeated maxim has applied to a variety of London brewers such as Truman, Watney, and Worthington, who have all shut up shop in the capital city. Fuller's, though, still occupies a pristine position by the Thames, owned and managed by the same families who have been in place for over 150 years. There is continuity in the site as well. The Griffin brewery has been around in one shape or another for well over 300 years.

Classic capital beers such as London Pride (4.1%) and ESB (5.5%) are brewed, the latter being one of the few English strong ales regularly produced by a family brewery. As with all great beers, balance is at the heart of the success of Fuller's beers. London Pride boasts a harmonic collaboration between grainy, biscuity malt and floral, citrusy hops, while ESB is a complex coalition of biscuity malt, rich orange citrus fruit and a dry, bitter finish. Fuller's also make a noted London Porter (5%), sturdy barley wine, Golden Pride (8.5%), and a bottle-conditioned strong ale, 1845 (6.3%). Meanwhile, the connoisseur market is catered for by the annual release of Vintage Ale (8.5%), a strong bottle-conditioned beer which is meant to be kept – if you can resist it. The vintages go back to 1997, when the then head brewer, Reg Drury, was given the chance to produce something special. He looked to the Golden Pride, then as now produced in non bottle-condition form, for his template and the brewery hasn't looked back since. John Keeling is now the head brewer and he has continued with the vintages, which all show great complexity as they age. Truly a grand cru of ales.

Gale's Brewery, *Horndean, Hampshire*

Back in the 1930s, the head brewer of this long-established family firm decided to make an end of it by jumping into a full fermenting vessel. According to the story, he put his pocket book and stop-watch on the side before leaping to his beery doom. Jokers say that that's why the brewery calls their beers full-bodied, but Gale's are noted for more than a bizarre suicide. They have been brewing beer on this site since the middle of the 19th century and their Victorian tower brewery is a marvel of economy and tradition. High up in the building, you will find the miller hard at work, watching the production of the grist. The noise is deafening, the mill is a flurry of belts and there is a powdery feel to the air. Another part of the brewery reveals the sampling room where the head brewer and his team sample beer at various times throughout the day. Even though there is plenty of noise and space is tight and lots of beer is being brewed, Gale's, like a lot of breweries, is almost a ghost ship in terms of people seen. Every corner turned has its surprises though. In the old coopering shop, which closed in 1967, you might find a small group of licensees being taken round by a blue-jacketed tour guide. In another room, more of Gale's licensees are busy in the middle of a British Institute of Innkeeping exam. The brewery takes its responsibility to the beer drinker seriously.

As for the beers, HSB (4.8%) is Gale's famous strong bitter with its good balance of rich malt flavours and aromas and hop fruitiness, while Festival Mild (4.8%) is a rare example of a strong mild. A local favourite that rarely travels outside the area is Butser Bitter (3.4%), a malt-accented session beer which is sprightly and delicious. However, for the beer connoisseur, the Gale's beer that rates the most mentions is their old-style barley wine – Prize Old Ale (9%), still produced in a corked bottle. This is a rich and complex beer that improves with age, and no beer collection should be without a brace.

Ridley's Brewery, *Hartford End, Essex*

The heart skips a beat when Ridley's Victorian brewery hoves into sight. Round a bend on a lonely country road, down a dip, and there it is, alongside the River Chelmer – a heart-stoppingly beautiful relic of Victorian brewing with a brick chimney, tower and huddle of roofs and buildings in the middle of rural contentment. Brewing started in 1842 and, until 2005, Ridley's was still owned by the eponymous family – one of whose ancestors was Bishop Nicholas Ridley, burnt at the stake during the reign of Bloody Mary. This was an event commemorated by Ridley's bottled Bishop's Ale, a powerful barley wine.

The pubs here are mainly country pubs, where locals gather to chat and ponder over the characteristics of Ridley's beers such as IPA, Rumpus and Old Bob. The man responsible for these handsomely crafted beers is Philip Downes, a passionate and informed beer-lover who has also worked at SA Brain and St Peters. 'When I was young I just decided I was going to be a brewer,' he says. 'I blame it on my mum who fed me a lot of malt extract. I often think it was that that turned me into a brewer.' Try a glass of Old Bob (5.2%), a strong bitter whose nose positively pulsates with the aromas of grainy, cereally malt before a bouquet of fruity and floral hoppy scent make their presence felt. The palate is just as well balanced. Caramel and sweet and juicy malt lead the unwary drinker on before the onset of fresh and fruity hoppy flavours. The finish is bittersweet with a lingering dryness.

SADLY, RIDLEY'S WAS CLOSED BY ITS NEW OWNERS GREENE KING IN 2005 AND THIS STANDS AS ITS EPITAPH.

G Schneider & Sohn, *Kelheim, Bavaria, Germany*
The latest member of the Schneider family is Georg VII who was born in 1995 and reputedly said the words Schneider Weisse the first time he spoke. Such a development is entirely in character with this world-famous dynasty of Bavarian wheat beer brewers. It all began in Munich in 1850, when Georg Schneider I was first given permission by the Bavarian King Ludwig I (whose statue now stands proud outside the current home) to make wheat beer. Prior to this, it was a privilege previously only allowed to the royal family, while the rest of society had to make do with murky brown-coloured ales. The capital of Bavaria was the Schneider home through revolution, coups and two world wars, the latter of which saw it destroyed in a bombing raid. In the late 1940s, the Schneider family moved north of Munich to the medieval town of Kelheim, which stands on the Danube and in the centre of the Hallertau hop-growing area. Georg Schneider IV had brought the brewhouse in the 1920s. It was built in 1607, which makes it one of the oldest establishments making beer in the world. A visit amid its stainless steel vessels, marble floors and unique architecture prepares the ground for uncovering the mystery of the sumptuously fruity and spicy Schneider Weisse (5.4%), whose recipe dates from 1864 and is still zealously guarded by the family. Strange as it might seem to us now as we enjoy wheat beers from Germany, Belgium, Britain, America and even Italy, the Bavarian Weisse was a style of beer which, until the 1980s, was seen by local beer-drinkers as the tipple of the aged and unfashionable. Since then, wheat beer sales have rocketed in Germany and Schneider have been able to ride that particular

trend. Gold-honeyed in colour, Schneider Weisse has an aroma of cloves, bananas and a hint of vanilla, while on the palate there are more bananas, cloves, a custard-like sweetness and a hint of bubblegum, before its descent into a tingling, fruity finish. The brewery is also known for its Doppel Bock Aventinus (8.2%), a rich, dark and strong wheat beer to be taken very seriously. Try both these beers at the Weissen Brauhaus, a few minutes from the brewery.

Sierra Nevada Brewing Company,
Chico, California, USA
Students taking up their studies in the university town of Chico could be seen as some of the luckiest in the world, for this is the home of one of the pioneering American microbreweries, Sierra Nevada. Since being set up in 1981 by avid home-brewer Ken Grossman and Paul Camusi, who used a selection of old dairy vessels, its beers have crossed the divide from micro to full-scale regional brewery. These days, the likes of its Pale Ale, Big Foot Barley Wine and Summerfest lager can be found throughout the United States and over the Atlantic in Britain. In 1989 Sierra Nevada moved to a sparkling new brewhouse full of steel vessels and up-to-date computer technology, where tours of hopheads wind their way around the fermenters inhaling all those delicious aromas. Afterwards, the Sierra Nevada Taproom is the place to try brewery-fresh beers as well as some excellent food. Sierra Nevada's Pale Ale (5.6%) is its signature beer, a style that has been much copied by American craft brewers and beyond. Dark gold in colour, the Pale Ale has a fresh fruity nose majoring in gorgeous hop notes, as if you had put your head in a hop sack in the brewery. The classic American hop Cascade is thrown into the boil as an aroma hop, which delivers this abundance of fruitiness. On the palate it has a smooth mouth-feel while a bready, cereal-like maltiness and tropical fruit notes (lychee) vie for the drinker's attention. The finish lasts with more cereal-like maltiness and bags of fruit making their return. It is a sumptuous banquet of a beer. Let nothing detract from Sierre Nevada's other beers though, as they also produce a Porter (5.6%), a Stout (5.8%), the summery lager called Summerfest (5%), the big-hearted barley wine Bigfoot (9.6%) and a spicy winter beer called Celebration (6.8%). And with beers like this, Sierra Nevada is truly a brewery to celebrate.

BREWERY PROFILE

St Austell Brewery, St Austell, Cornwall

The Cornish like their beer and like their beer to be Cornish. At the last count there were 15 breweries of all shapes and sizes in Cornwall. Most trade on their Cornish heritage but none thankfully look back as far as the 16th century when Cornish beer was described as 'looking white and thick as if pigs had wrestled in it'. The great grandfather of all Cornish breweries is St Austell, which has been brewing since the 1870s, when local maltster William Hicks (below) started supplying beer to the thirsty mining community.

Today, the sight of the magnificent Victorian tower brewery at the top of the town is a visible reminder of Hicks' foresight. Brewing at St Austell still works on the principles of a traditional tower brewery – just as it was planned in the 19th century.

Beer-making starts high up in a small room at the top, where malt is crushed by a mill after being delivered up there from a grain silo. On the next level below is the mashing room, where a couple of stately looking mash tuns with copper facings hold the grist for St Austell's beers. Inside there will be a mass of crushed, well-soaked grain from which the precious wort is being extracted. Next stop is the brewing copper where whole-leaf hops are added to the wort for bitterness and aroma.

Head brewer Roger Ryman, who joined the company from Maclays in 1999, uses four hop varieties for his regulars – Fuggles, Goldings, Willamette, Styrian Goldings – though others are picked for any specialist beers he makes. In the fermenting rooms 12 black-and-white vessels hold the beer in the uneasy sleep of fermentation. Even though St Austell positively reeks of tradition, with lots of shining copper, brass fittings and low beams, time does not stand still. 'We are proud of our heritage but not stuck in the past,' says Roger Ryman, who has always been keen to introduce new flavours and brewing techniques. The company's innovative wheat beer Clouded Yellow came out of a beer especially brewed for the 1999 Celtic Beer Festival, which St Austell host

each December. At 2004's festival, Ryman had the brewery's bestselling Tribute maturing in an old sour mash whisky barrel, while their rare and wonderful barley wine Smugglers Ale sat quietly and contemplative in a former rum barrel. Both were stupendous beers with the Tribute Extra boasting plenty of buttery, vanilla notes and a long lush finish, while the Smugglers had a great oaky vigour, sweetness and plenty of drinkability. All these beers emanate from Ryman's small microbrewery which is often pressed into service throughout the year. On the regular

side, the brewery's golden beer Tribute (4.2%) has been winning the plaudits, sales and awards (in 2004 it was CAMRA Champion Beer of Cornwall). And what a beer it is; a gorgeously aromatic golden beer which is boosted by the presence of the gloriously fruity hop Cascade in the mix. Cornish beer has come a long way from wrestling pigs.

BREWPUBS

FROM TUN TO GLASS

The brewpub has a long history in Great Britain. During the 19th century thousands of licensees made their own beer, but most of them were devoured by growing family brewing firms hungry for premises to push out their 'running beers', the early versions of today's bitter. This decline continued throughout the 20th century until a hardy band of four stood alone in the early 1970s. The end of the brewpub seemed nigh and that faded artwork on the side of a wall promising home-brewed ales was all that would remain. Fortunately this was not to be. Times change and there are now dozens of pubs whose licensees have set up a stainless steel brewing kit in an old stable block, garage or even inside the pub. Sometimes, brewing takes place during opening hours and drinkers can see how their pint came into being. Like a lot of great ideas, the brewpub has travelled the world. Whether it is in Prague, where U Fleků dates back to the Middle Ages, or the Bavarian town of Bamberg which produces its unique Rauchbier, or newer establishments in Italy, the USA or even Columbia, the brewpub is a sign of good beer. For the discerning licensee, brewing your own beer is a sign of passion and pride in your product.

Below: the view outside and inside the Old Cannon Brewpub in Bury St Edmunds.

Leith Hill, *Coldharbour, near Dorking, Surrey*
At one stage in its history, Leith Hill was one of the tiniest micros in the land. When I visited in 1998, two years after it had opened, it looked like a plastic bin was doing time as a fermenting vessel, thus enabling the brewer to produce nine gallons each brew. Size isn't everything though as it didn't make any difference to the two beers I tasted in the Plough, the pub where the brewery is based. Crooked Furrow (4%) was a fruity and refreshing best bitter, while Tallywhacker (5.6%) was an absurdly delicious strong dark beer with plenty of malt character. Times have changed and the brewery is now a two-barrel operation. Its beers make a welcome reward at the Plough after a solid walk on nearby Leith Hill.

Trossachs Craft, *Kilmahog, Scotland*
The first Ben of the Highlands, Ben Ledi, overlooks the small village of Kilmahog. The community is also home to the Lade Inn, a former coaching inn, where Trossachs Craft started brewing in 2003. The brewery is situated in an old garage. According to

licensee Jill Nixon, 'We were approached by the now brewer who said that the space was being wasted and could be used for a brewery. We had been thinking of what to do with the garage and a brewery seemed a good idea.' The beers, such as Waylade (3.9%) and Ladeback (4.5%), are exclusively organic and sold only in the pub. What better way to celebrate the start of the Highlands than with a local ale.

Six Bells, *Bishops Castle, Shropshire*
Not content with a brewery at the top of town (the John Roberts at the Three Tuns), Bishops Castle also has the Six Bells at the bottom of the high street, where landlord Neville Richards runs a five-barrel operation in the pub's former stables. Welshman Neville has brewing form (his grandfather once ran a brewery), which may account for the popularity of his hoppy beers. They are, naturally, found at the bar of the Six Bells as well as in several other pubs in the area. 'I think every pub should have its own angle,' says Neville, 'and this is mine.'

The Blue Anchor, *Helston, Cornwall*
The Blue Anchor is a legend in its own lifetime. Brewing has taken place at this venerable pub for nearly 200 years now according to landlord Simon Stone, who has been its custodian since 1993. However, as the site was once occupied by monks who ran a medieval guest house, there's a chance that brewing beer on-site goes back many more centuries. The brewery is at the back of the pub, which remains a warren of small rooms with ancient wooden furniture; a place where time is elastic. People have been known to pop in for a quick drink and spend the whole day there. Others have been known to move to Helston to be nearer. The beers have the generic name of Spingo and are noted for their strength, with popular regulars Middle and Special weighing in at 5% and 6.6% respectively. As if to make matters even more exciting, brewer Tim Sears produces an even stronger beer for Easter and Christmas. The Blue Anchor is a national treasure and if you only ever visit one brewpub, this is the place.

WISHING YOU WERE HERE

BREWERIES IN PICTURE-POSTCARD PLACES

Thornbridge Brewery,
Ashford in the Water, Derbyshire

A trip to Thornbridge Brewery, based at Thornbridge Hall (right) in the village of Ashford in the Water, is as much a visit to the land of *Homes & Gardens*, as it is to see and taste the fruits of John Barleycorn. The Hall boasts sweeping staircases, high-ceilinged rooms, gorgeous views over ornate gardens and windows by William Morris and Edward Byrne-Jones. It also houses a new 10-barrel brewery which has been set up by local businessman Jim Harrison (who owns the house with wife and entrepreneur Emma), along with Dave Wickett, the owner of the Fat Cat pub and its adjoining Kelham Island Brewery in Sheffield. Initially used to brew Kelham Island ales to cope with increased orders after Pale Rider's championship title at Olympia 2005, the brewery is now producing Thornbridge's own brews including Craven Silk, an aromatic, rich and fruity session bitter at 4% whose palate is enlivened by the addition of elderflower into the mix. The elderflower is part of Jim's brewing plans as he hopes to use other herbs, flowers and fruits from the estate to create Thornbridge's special beers.

Branscombe Vale, *Branscombe, Devon*

Brewers Graham Luxton and Paul Dimond make their wonderful beers in old farm buildings leased from the National Trust. The South West Coast path passes by their front door so if they ever get bored they can look out over the sea and watch its ever-changing moods. The beautiful village of Branscombe is also close, which is just as well as the Fountain Head, found at the other end of this elongated settlement, is the unofficial brewery tap for Branscombe Vale. Set up in 1992, Branscombe has become a substantial force on the South Devon coast with beers such as Branoc Bitter, Summa That and Drayman's Best Bitter flying out of the brewery's window.

St Peter's Brewery, *near Bungay, Suffolk*

A hare runs across a field, the arc of a rainbow is visible in the distance, ducks sit and quack on a small island in the middle of a moat in front of an old medieval manor house. Seen for the first time from across the fields, this is jaw-droppingly pretty scene worthy of the very best of a television costume drama. However, behind the manor house, beer is being brewed. Welcome to St Peter's Brewery in the Suffolk flatlands south of Bungay, where old barns have been converted to a brewery and bottling plant. The manor house is a restaurant where good food can be sampled alongside a stunning range of beers, which include ones made with grapefruit, honey, lemon and ginger and even nettles. These may sound outrageous, but the skills of the brewers ensure a delicious balance of flavours that is still beer. More conventional ales include a 3.7% Best Bitter and a stupendous 6.5% Cream Stout, which sings with roast coffee and chocolate aromas. In the autumn of 2005, it was reported that the brewery was for sale. It is to be hoped that brewing will continue at such a beautiful site.

Plzensky Prazdroj, Plzen, Czech Republic

Main Street Disneyland seems to have turned up in one of the world's most famous breweries, just as you've entered through a portal that resembles a miniature of the Brandenburg Gate in Berlin. As befitting the original home of real lager, the surroundings of the Pilsner Urquell brewery in Plzen (or Pilsen) are somewhat larger than life. Glance around: a massive locomotive sits undercover, not far from what looks like a minaret from 1001 Arabian Nights but is in fact a water tower. Down beneath the brewery, there are nine kilometres of tunnel, which were dug in the soft sandstone during the 19th century. Here, in these underground passageways, pitch-lined barrels of lager used to be left to mature before going out to conquer the world and becoming the prototype for all the golden beers that have been brewed since.

This is brewing as tourism with over 250,000 souls visiting the site each year for a tour that takes in a film, artefacts, a visit around the brewhouse and a tasting of the beer from wooden barrels in the subterranean cellars – unfiltered and unpasteurised with striking hints of banana and cloves, characteristics usually noted in German Weisse.

Plzen's Pilsner fame stretches back to 1842 when the local brewers combined to purge their town's poor brewing reputation by commissioning Bavarian brewer Josef Groll to make their beer. By accident or design, Groll came up with a golden-coloured bottom-fermented beer, which first of all conquered Prague and then spread out through the world. In 1898, the trademark *Pilsner Urquell* (meaning Pilsner from the original source) was registered to try and forestall the many imitators, and the name remains to this day.

In the mid-1990s, after the company had loosened the shackles of the state, Pilsner Urquell dropped the old style of fermentation and plumped for stainless steel conical fermenters. The period of maturation was also shortened, which some felt affected the complexity of the beer. Understandably, there's a romance about oak barrels sitting quietly in the dark beneath the earth, but brewing seldom has time for that sort of thing when there are customers clamouring for beer all over the world, as there are with Pilsner Urquell. Now the company is owned by global brewers SAB-Miller, who also brew it in Poland and Russia, with the triple decoction method and same raw materials to hand under the beady scrutiny of a Plzen brewmaster. However, whatever the doubts, and some beer-lovers do have them, Pilsner Urquell still remains a great beer and a visit to Plzen is a must for every serious lover of beer.

Pilsner Urquell (4.4%)

Saaz hops, in pellet form (flower hops were used until the early 1990s), plus hop oil, which apparently has similar characteristics to the German hop Perle, are combined with lightly cured Pilsner malt, while the beer matures for 30 days. Expect a soft malt and resiny hop nose, while the palate is rounded with a light hop bitterness, followed by a long dry finish. Intriguingly enough the Polish Pilsner Urquell has more hop on the palate plus a distinctive hint of butterscotch (diacetyl in brewing terms) on the nose.

WOMEN AND BEER

Fem'ale

Women have raised a glass (or earthenware pot) of cheer for thousands of years. The Ancient Babylonians even worshipped beer in the female form of the goddess Ninkasi. In the Middle Ages women, or brewsters as they were called, were mainly responsible for the making of ale, and woe betide any of these alewives if they got their beer wrong. A ducking in the local village pond usually beckoned. Nearer to our time, in the immediate aftermath of the Second World War and the social upheaval caused by the large scale entry of women into the work-place, it was noted that young women were downing pints. Postwar attitudes developed with the belief that the public bar was not a fit place for a 'lady', unless she sat quietly in the corner sipping a port and lemon.

However, the last few years have seen plenty of change as women muscle their way back to the bar, stand sentinel at the mash tun and make decisions in managerial positions at all levels in the brewing industry. The Brewing Research International has an all-woman panel of trained beer tasters, CAMRA claims that women make up over 25% of its membership, while many bars and pubs have to keep women in mind if they want to succeed. 'There are definitely more women drinking beer,' says Sara Barton at Brewster's. 'I think a lot of them have come in through the Belgium beer route. Lots of pubs are opening up, becoming roomier, there are not so many dark and smoky ones. Bars are popular but you don't get the real ale into them. We need to try and sell real ale in the same way as a quality wine like Bordeaux. Show women that they can drink it with a meal – there are lots of beers that will go with different courses. I like cherry kriek with chocolate cake, it's almost like a dessert beer. In some ways there is still a macho attitude towards drinking beer, that it has to be downed in lots of pints. It doesn't.'

Despite breweries' insistence to the contrary, it does seem that the launch of so many beers flavoured with fruit, honey, chocolate and other things sweet (usually seen as the way to a woman's palate) is a direct pitch for the female drinker. One head brewer

at an old family firm confessed as much to me when we were talking about a beer flavoured with tropical fruit. This stems from the fact that there has always been a perception that women beer drinkers dislike the aggressive hoppiness of English bitter. According to John Gilbert, the founder of Hop Back Brewery, 'I have a theory that when lager was being brewed in the UK in the 1960s the powers-that-be decided that too much hops would put off women, who were seen as the main market. That's rubbish, women and men have the same taste buds'.

Several years ago, the annual Beauty of Hops competition put women's taste buds to the challenge.

An all-female panel of brewers, distillers, sensory evaluators, beer retailers and journalists were asked to find Britain's most female friendly ale. According to the competition's organiser, Rupert Ponsonby, 'What was interesting was the main conclusion that women like sweetness in their beers, but only if it's backed up with other adjectives like chocolatey or honeyed. Sweetness on its own is no good – think of how we turn our noses up at a sweet white wine'.

Real beer is for everyone, whether it's a glass of raspberry wheat beer or a pint of well-hopped bitter. Some would say that given that men are from Mars and women are from Venus perhaps a bottle of Brutal Bitter for him and Cantillon Rose for her means that the old distinctions still exist, but the sight at a beer festival of CAMRA male stalwarts enjoying a delicate fruit beer, while female newcomers to the grain tuck into an East Anglian best bitter suggests that the only thing the sexes agree on is the joy of good beer.

If you like Barcardi Breezer or Wicked, try a fruit beer from St Peters in Suffolk or Liefman's classic Kriek or Framboise fruit beers. If you like a glass of Chardonnay, try a Pale Rider from Kelham Island, or a Bitter & Twisted from Harviestoun. Both are golden beers with light delicate hop-fruit aromas and flavours.

BEER PEOPLE

Belinda Sutton, Elgood's

Belinda Sutton is Managing Director of family brewers Elgood's, of Wisbech, Cambridgeshire.

'You could say that the industry chose me, as I was born into it. Mine is the fifth generation of the Elgood family to be involved in brewing and I always wanted to be a part of it. However, I have found it to be a male-oriented business. The first time I encountered this properly was at an IFBB (Independent Family Brewers of Britain) meeting at the Brewers' Society offices, then in Portman Square. I arrived with my father to meet all the other family brewers, and was asked first if I could fetch someone a drink and then for directions to the gents' toilets. Both times I had been mistaken for someone who worked in the building, rather than as a member of the brewing industry!

It's different whenever I visit one of our landlords, they know who to expect and never show surprise. However, I would say that our free-trade sales team seem to get a positive response to a woman running the brewery – just because it is different, I suppose!

I like just about everything in the brewing business. I enjoy producing and making new beers, and I enjoy visiting the pubs and meeting the tenants. I like the fact that all the brewers are friendly and talk to one another and it is a very sociable business to be in. I also find that everyone treats each other with respect, which is nice to see these days. One thing I do dislike is the way the industry as a whole is cast as the bad guy by the media. It always seems to be 'the big bad brewers' who get the blame for everything from high prices to binge drinking! I am also occasionally irritated when people are surprised by the fact that women are involved in the industry at every level; after all, in times gone by brewing was considered to be almost exclusively women's work!

Among the high spots of being at Elgood's would definitely be our bi-centenary celebrations in 1995, when we had a whole week of celebrations for family, staff and customers. More recently, we have acquired three new pubs, The Waggon & Horses in Cambridge, Floods Tavern in St Ives, and The Reindeer in Norwich. Each pub-opening has been a great event, and we aim to continue to acquire new premises whenever something suitable becomes available.

I very much enjoy working for Elgood's. We have a wonderful team of people here. I meet very nice people, both within our tied estate and at beer festivals and other events. It is a fascinating industry, with very exciting challenges, and, as I said before, I was brought up to love it, and hope to continue for a long time to come.'

Right: Elgood's Belinda Sutton with her father Nigel Stewart Elgood.

BEER PEOPLE

Susan Simpson, Brown Cow Brewery

Susan Simpson runs the Brown Cow Brewery in a former riverside inn outside Selby in North Yorkshire

'My first interest was in home-brewing for a hobby, which started about 15 years ago, but I decided to take the leap into commercial brewing in 1997. After spending 18 years desk-bound in a 9–5 job I was made redundant and in a position to change my working life. I didn't want to go back to an office job and ideally wanted to run a small business from home. Something I had once read had stuck with me and that was if you could turn what you enjoyed doing as a hobby into a business then you would be happy in your work. I am a reasonably practical and creative type of person so decided to give it a go.

The first seeds were sown in 1996 taking advice from various sources; brewing consultants, other small brewers, potential customers and the local planning department. My husband was at that time working all over the country and would spend time away from home so it was vital that I did my homework to make sure it was feasible for me to work on my own most of the time otherwise I would fall flat on my face at the first hurdle. I also realised it was too big a leap to go from home brewing to brewing commercially and enlisted a brewing consultant to supply my first plant (two and a half barrels) and teach me to brew. So in 1997 after watching the consultant brew for a day, he then supervised me brewing the next day. I then flew solo with telephone support if needed (which of course I did), but got through relatively unscathed! The first year or so was fraught with all sorts of difficulties – it was also physically much harder than I had anticipated and I felt like giving up many times but wanted to prove the 'she'll never do it' brigade wrong (stubborn woman syndrome!).

I would say most landlords are surprised to discover that I am the brewer but am glad to say I have never had any negative vibes, just genuine interest. In small-scale craft brewing I have found that generally the people you meet, both customers and fellow brewers, all share the same enthusiasm and pride regarding what they do and the promotion of real ale. It's also great to have a job that most people seem genuinely interested in. When people ask what I do they always have questions to ask and their eyes don't glaze over (which was most people's reaction to my previous job of Computer Customer Service Help Desk Operator!).

I am always thrilled to bits whenever a beer picks up an award at a festival, and one high spot was overhearing "by-eck, that lass can mek a gud pint!"'

'I'm not sure about whether women prefer different beers from men, though if pressed I would say no. Everybody's palate, whether male or female, is very individual and subjective – thank goodness or there would only be the need to brew one beer that would suit everybody. From a personal point of view, I enjoy a beer with a quite a hefty bittering level and find the time of year can affect the type of beer I choose.'

SUSAN SIMPSON
Brown Cow Brewery

BEER PEOPLE

Liz O'Hanlon, O'Hanlon's Brewery Company

Liz O'Hanlon owns and runs Hanlon's Brewery with husband John O'Hanlon and is based near the village of Whimple outside Exeter, Devon.

'My background is sales, while John's is in pubs. We had the pub O'Hanlon's in Clerkenwell, London, which John ran while I was working elsewhere. We had been living in Oxfordshire, brewing in Vauxhall, and our pub was in Clerkenwell, and we decided it was all getting too complicated. The brewery was going well but we needed to spend more time with it, so we decided to put all our eggs into one basket.

Moving out here was a long hard slog. A lot of research on the property had to be done before we could place a bid. We had to check the water supply, which is supplied by a well, and we had a diviner in to check that there was a secondary source just in case the first one dried up; and also that the water was satisfactory for making beer. It was a risk but we placed our bid and were successful. Then we had to apply for planning permission, which was declined initially, but eventually we got it. We moved here in July 2000 and by end of November 2000 we started brewing.

When we set up the brewing business I went into it to look after the sales operations. The brewing industry was different from what I was used to. It was very friendly from the start and being a woman has never been an issue. Maybe the fact that I had the name of the company helped. First and foremost as a representative of the business I find everyone friendly, whether they are pub owner, supermarket beer buyer or wholesaler. Everyone has been completely helpful. Maybe it was different for women 20 years ago.

It has been a huge challenge to put our name on the map, to go from being small fry to be noticed, but on the other hand we enjoy a challenge. High spots have been the awards, especially the Champion Bottle-Conditioned Beer of Great Britain, which we won with Port Stout in 2003. It changed our profile and accelerated our export sales. Being awarded the license to brew Royal Oak and the Thomas Hardy's Ale was also a real challenge for us and it changed the complexion of the brewery. The brewing of Thomas Hardy takes several months with the beer being tied up in fermenting vessels for some time so we needed more storage.

I enjoy a beer and have always liked the golden ales but I also like a stout now and again. Our wheat beer is also very female friendly.

I face the same demands on my time as any other working mother. You always have to juggle things with children, horses and dogs, but working together as a husband and wife team helps to share the load.'

DRINKING BEER

In a **PUB** or **bar**, with friends or
in silent contemplation, **a glass of real beer**
is always a pleasure to be savoured.
DRINKING BEER brings to life
the many facets of this great drink
and the places where it is enjoyed.

FANCY A BEER?

CALLED TO THE BAR

Drinking fresh beer wherever you are in the world is a joyous experience, and the best place to sample it is the pub, bar or café. Beer at home has its place, a bottle of barley wine before bed, a thirst-quenching golden ale while standing guard at the barbecue, but beer is best in the company of others. Across the world, from kellers in Germany, to pristine brewpubs for hop-heads in America, beer cafés in Belgium and crowded pubs in the Czech Republic, these are the places where drinking the local brew can open doors to new tastes and new people. Nowhere else in the world is there a place that offers so much for so many. It's the place to do business, to network and cut deals. Equally, it's a place to unwind and relax; a home from home or a home to escape home. It's a place to have a good laugh or cry on a friend's shoulder when things get too much. The home of fresh beer generates a feeling of belonging as soon as the threshold is crossed. A nod and a smile from regulars at the bar can soothe stressed hearts; inclusion not exclusion – we all need it. You can meet your mates at the bar or you might even find your future mate, eyes meeting across a crowded room!

Pubs, kellers, café bars – call them what you will: if they don't have decent beer and a welcoming person serving the beer and keeping a good house, they aren't worthy of the name. Good cellarmanship is the drinks' equivalent of a Michelin-starred chef taking pride in his kitchen, whether it's the local beer on tap served immaculately or a chalked up sign in a brewpub offering the week's specialities, this is a sight to gladden the heart. Good beer and good food go together as well – smoked cheese, cold meat and sweet mustard in a Czech tavern, the beer cuisine of a Belgian café bar or a Tex-Mex platter of a Boston brewpub. It's not just the food and drink that count either. The home of good beer can also have a sense of history – U Fleků in Prague is the sole survivor of the city's once thriving tradition of brewpubs; celebrate the fin de siècle style of the Mort Subite in Brussels or enjoy the tradition of Bamberg's unique *Rauchbier* (smoked beer) at the Schlenkerla Tavern.

THE PUB'S THE PLACE

WHAT IS A PUB?

The British pub is utterly unique. Some are gloriously and stubbornly old-fashioned: dark, cloistered palaces dedicated to the arcane art of drinking, where the snug has survived the attentions of those eminent Victorians who thought it a home to vice. These are the kind of pubs that thrive on tradition. A sense of continuity and history resonates from the pictures and prints that cover the walls. The best of these pubs is a bulwark against the froth and wash of modern life, without turning into a false and fraudulent celebration of the 'good old days'. Thrive on tradition, yes, but acknowledge changing times.

Other pubs are fresh and bright, upbeat and eager with light pouring in; all the better to appreciate the sparkle of a golden beer in its glass. Expect cosy sofas, stripped pine furniture, beers from home and abroad, and food with an accent on the unusual. Whether old, middle-aged or new, a good pub is a comfort, a crossroads of social mobility, a centre of communications and a place where the reward of a great beer sustains during the long working day. There are town pubs, city pubs, suburban pubs, seaside pubs, village pubs, in the middle-of-nowhere pubs, pub pubs, and brewpubs where the beer is freshly brewed on the premises. Each will be quite different, each will have its own unique atmosphere. But one thing that binds all good pubs together is that they are the heartbeat of a community; as well as being a home of good beer.

The rural local brings people together. It's the place where gossip is swapped, tall tales are told and there's always the chance of bumping into someone you know. If you're lucky, all this can be accompanied with several pints of a local beer brewed down the road. For the regular, the village pub is business, pleasure and social duty all rolled into one. For the visitor, a pint in the corner of a country pub is nirvana. It brings a chance for idle contemplation, people-watching or simply gazing out of the window and letting the world drift by. In a fast-moving society, we all need to slow down and stop what we are doing: slow drink, slow food, slow life. Pubs are the ideal one-stop shops where time and a good pint can be bought with a minimum of fuss. Village pubs are also public services. Some sell newspapers, especially on a Sunday, or act as a post-office. Others provide rooms for local groups of like-minded souls to meet. Hush, the cricket team has its AGM tonight, while tomorrow morning sees the Parish Council in action.

In cities and towns, the world outside the pub is more frenetic, but inside time stands reassuringly still. No one talks to you in a modern café where the chrome is more polished than the food, but visit most good city pubs and (should you wish) you're bound to end up in conversation with one of the locals. Cities, unfriendly places? Not if you're sitting in a pub with a pint. From London to Liverpool, from Sheffield to Stromness, all is grist to the mill of discussion, from the fortunes of favourite football clubs, to the quality of the beer, the duplicity of politicians and, of course, that great British obsession, the weather.

The first pub? Back in the Dark Ages, for sure. Certainly as soon as the Romans arrived they ordered wayside inns (or *tabernae*) to be built alongside their new straight roads. In those far-off days, it was a handy pit-stop for food and fuel if you were travelling up-country in a chariot. The Saxons

and all the other folk from over the northern seas brought in toasts and enjoyed nothing better than a good night of wassailing, after a hard day spent rampaging through the countryside causing all sorts of mayhem (a kind of binge-drinking in reverse). Come medieval times, the monks took over, running their own hostelries where weary travellers could stop for a bite and a pint and a quick look at an illustrated scroll. Taverns in the town acted as a home from home for anyone sick of looking at the four walls of their wattle and daub hovel. Coaching inns provided warmth and vittles for travellers when crossing countries and borders in comfort was

In a fast-moving society, we all need to slow down and enjoy time and friends; the pub is ideal for this.

unheard of. Victorian gin palaces made drinkers feel like royalty amid the opulence of engraved glass, polished brass and fluttering gas lamps, much to the dismay of temperance campaigners, who set up their own alternative establishments serving tea and soft drinks. Nowadays even royalty have been known to come to the pub to pull a pint.

Two thousand years after the first pubs set up shop, drinkers are still being welcomed into their hallowed confines. Other countries may have the *keller*, *birreria* or bar, but the British have the pub and for that give many thanks.

A NOT-TOTALLY-SERIOUS-HISTORY OF THE PUB

AD 43 Romans invade Britain and set up the first taverns. Soldiers on garrison duty are supplied by local brewers.

410 Romans leave Britons to their own devices. Angles, Saxons and Jutes start arriving, bringing their drinking horns with them.

688 Laws are passed by King Ina of Wessex to set up alehouses as successors to the Roman taverns.

745 Top clergyman, Ecbright, Archbishop of York, bans priests from going to alehouses.

793 King Offa of Mercia founds a monastery in St Albans which becomes Ye Old Fighting Cocks, England's oldest pub.

1129 A German ambassador to Norman England writes that 'the Inns of England are the best in Europe'.

1189 Nottingham pub Ye Olde Trip To Jerusalem acts as a staging post for Crusaders on their way to cause havoc in the Middle East. It still serves beer.

1380s Geoffrey Chaucer writes the *Canterbury Tales* which tells of a group of pilgrims meeting at the Tabard Inn in south London.

1393 London landlords are ordered to display signs outside their establishments.

1500s Hopped beer starts coming into vogue.

1550 Closing time is fixed at 9pm in the summer and 8pm in the winter.

1720s Porter allegedly comes into being.

1742 Whitbread starts brewing and four years later has 13 tied houses.

1785 The beer pump handle is patented by British inventor Joseph Bramah.

1830 The Beer House Act is passed which makes it easier to open pubs, much to the dismay of the growing teetotaller movement. The Act is amended in 1834.

1853 Sunday pub closing introduced in Scotland. Wales follows in 1881.

1892 A throwaway paper mat for a glass to rest on is patented in Germany. The beer mat or coaster reaches Britain by the 1920s.

1915 The Defence of the Realm Act is passed with restrictions on opening hours, many of which aren't changed until the 1980s.

1920 The 'noble experiment' of Prohibition comes into force in the USA, boosting criminal fortunes until its demise in 1933.

1922 A Bavarian landlord runs short of beer and adds lemonade to the mix, inventing *radler* or shandy.

1950s Pump clips start to appear on handpumps in British pubs.

1953 First keg beer is sent out to British pubs.

1970s This is the decade of pub 'modernisation' where many traditional pubs were gutted, knocked through and themed.

1971 The Campaign for Real Ale is formed to lobby for traditional pubs and cask-conditioned beer.

1977 All-day opening and Sunday opening appear in Scotland.

1980s-present Continued growth in homebrew pubs, sadly equalled by the advancement of traditional pubs done up and done over into theme pubs with silly names.

1988 Pubs in England and Wales finally follow Scotland and are allowed to stay open all day. All-day Sunday opening followed in the mid-90s.

1990 The Beer Orders Act comes into being, with no one brewery allowed to have an estate of pubs larger than 2,000; the right of a brewery-owned pub to have a 'guest' cask ale is also introduced. Pub companies spring into being, some of them managed by former employees of the big pub-owning breweries.

2005 There are nearly 60,000 pubs in Britain with around half of them owned by pub companies.

BEER PEOPLE

'Why I make real beer' – the view from the mash tun

JOHN BRYAN, *Head Brewer, Oakham Ales, Peterborough*

John Bryan: his craft is such that he sports a tattoo of a hop on his arm.

'I have been here over nine years. I was home-brewing from aged 16 and also working on my father's farm. In my early 20s I was at the end of my tether and looking for different avenues. I had mad ideas like being a pilot but I really wanted to do something crafty. It came down to cheese-making or brewing. I had an ever-growing love of beer and I used to go to the Rose Tavern at Wisbech and the publican took me to a few breweries. On one of these trips I met John Woods, the then owner of Oakham. The cogs started turning and I befriended John and offered my help. Telling my father that I was not going to be following him into the farm was one of the worst things I have done.

My father was getting on and we sold up the farm and I asked John Woods if he would be interested in a partner buying into the brewery. However, he called back and asked if I would like to buy it. He was selling because of various reasons. At the time I couldn't so that was that. Next thing you know, my dad passed me a phone message about someone called Hook on a boat calling. I thought, 'Hook, boat, oh yeah' and threw it away. It turned out to be Paul Hook who had bought Oakham and he needed a brewer. My name was put forward. So after an interview, I got the job, went on a course and began brewing. It was a bit scary at first. We then moved from Oakham to Peterborough and we will soon be moving further to a site a couple of miles away which will be 70 barrels in brew length.

I have always been interested in pubs. I remember being taken to them when I was a kid and like a lot of people started off drinking cider because it was sweet. Then I tried lager, but when I started home-brewing real ale became my tipple. No matter what they say, those kits never work, so I looked to a full grain mash system. To be honest the silly names of real ale drew me into drinking it. It wasn't until my early 20s when I really loved my real ale.

Oakham started in 1993 and I joined two years later. Then it was 10 barrels a week and then went up to 30 barrels a week. When I won my first award for the beer I was more relaxed than anything else.

John Woods had won several awards but oddly enough I can't remember where the first one was, but I did think 'yes I'm doing it right'. At first it was hard, I was in the deep end so winning was a relief. My father used to have a go at me when I came second and ask why I didn't come first!

I brew to my own taste. That's all I've ever done. It is quite a varied taste. We have come up with a winning formula with the beers but I hope to sidetrack a bit and produce some different ones. We have been labelled as a golden beer brewery but in fact we do quite a large range. I like making balanced beers, but I also like extremities with loads of flavours. There are loads of flavours in hops and malt so why not get them into the beer.

I love the whole industry; get excited about brewhouses, especially Victorian ones. Stainless steel is a sexy material as well. The farming background gives me a connection with the malt side of things, a link with my past. I also love hops, hence the tattoo. That was done for the 10th anniversary of the brewery and it was also my father's birthday. I had the brewery's logo done in 2001.

My father is an old fenman and doesn't make a fuss about things. He's never really shown outward appreciation of what I've done, but I remember going round to his house and seeing pictures from when we won the champion beer on his wall. I was really chuffed.'

'Why I sell real beer' – the view from behind the bar

MARK DORBER, *the White Horse, Parson's Green, London*

Mark Dorber has been landlord at the White Horse for over 20 years (he also has a second pub, the Anchor in Walberswick, Suffolk). In that time, the White Horse has developed from being an ordinary Victorian corner boozer to a veritable temple of beer.

'I got turned on to beer by Burton-brewed Draught Bass. What got me interested in it was a combination of its inherent liveliness and the beautiful aromatics of the East Kent Goldings which it was dry hopped with, plus the very special properties of what were up to 13 different yeast strains working away.

I have always drunk beer. My Uncle Joe had a Wilson's pub in Salford and I remember wandering around his cellar with wooden hogsheads from the age or three or four. I delivered beer for Everards while at university and saw a lot of their country pubs. I drank a lot of Marston's Pedigree at university; sought out beer and supported CAMRA.'

Legend has it that Mark Dorber started off by working in the cellar of the pub on evenings after he'd spent the day working in the City. His passion for beer still burns within and he is a great apostle of treating beer with the reverence it deserves. Here is his ethos on good cellarmanship:

'I think it is important to show every beer at its very finest, which involves a personal judgment when every beer is at its personal best in terms of the amount of carbonation you build up and the age of the beer. That means you ought to dispense it relatively swiftly. The essence of great beer is drinking it when it's freshly broached. The first couple of hours yield that beer at its sublime best.

Bar staff should experiment and interpret and tell drinkers what they have done with the beers. If you have kept it for three weeks tell people, engage in discussion with your most discerning customers to agree when the best combination of flavours and aromas is most likely to appear. Get your customers to help you because in some cases they have better palates than you. I wouldn't presume to tell some of the locals in the Anchor how Adnams Best Bitter should taste because I haven't tasted it through the seasons like they have.

Don't stillage a beer unless it's at cellar temperature. Make sure you rouse the beer thoroughly before you stillage. Clean, shive and keystone thoroughly and soft peg immediately; don't allow the soft peg to be left in unattended for more than 15 minutes at a go when the beer has vented sufficiently. That is something you have to determine yourself according to the finings regime and everything else that operates. Hard peg and don't do it with one of these so-called wooden, semi-hard, semi-soft pegs. Use a plastic or non-porous hard peg to build up condition. Too much condition is being wafted into the cellars these days. Preserve condition, it's the life-force, it gives key mouth-feel and crucial lifeness and properties.'

IN SEARCH OF THE BRITISH PUB

Pub design should make drinkers feel at home, though few will enjoy a bar in their own living room or a snug off the kitchen. Although there are impersonal pubs that feature knick-knacks bought off-the-peg and large barn-like rooms with blaring music and designer drinks, there is now far more choice available. Look for the four essentially British styles of pub designed to make going out for a drink a pleasure.

VICTORIAN GEM

Grandness is second nature to this institution, built during the latter days of Queen Victoria's reign when brewers wanted their pubs to match the social aspirations of their clientele. From the outside the ornate building has the air of a municipal town hall more used to receiving the great, the good and the corrupt than those with a liking for ale. Sometimes a grand clock-tower dominates proceedings while the name of the pub might be picked out in stone. Inside there's a wealth of mahogany features, stained-glass and engraved windows and mirrors, as well as the now rarely seen 'snob screens', designed to keep the well-off from being seen by the hoi-polloi. The place fell on hard times in the 1970s and it might even have closed for a while, but a sympathetic brewery stepped in and returned it to its former glory. Good beer and food is always on tap.

TRY: **The Bartons Arms**, Birmingham; the **Lamb Tavern**, London; the **Philharmonic**, Liverpool.

POST-MODERNIST WATERING HOLE

Shop! Even though this single-roomed town or city pub looks like it's been around for ever, it was once a grocery, hardware store or even a bakery until its recent award-winning conversion. Unlike theme bar change-overs, where former department stores or car showrooms get turned into soulless barns for perpendicular drinking, this post-modernist pub has a style that mixes and matches the best of old and new. Expect oak floors, a wooden bar; gleaming, well-polished brass fittings and stainless steel handpumps; sometimes the beer is served straight from the cellar. Light is important and will be encouraged in by a large glass frontage (no hiding away from the world here) and reflected by old-style brewery mirrors. Beer memorabilia such as framed posters, award certificates, pump clips of past beers and old arty black-and-white photo displays, will gladden the heart of ale-lovers with a sense of style. Some pubs (especially those in rural areas) may have old photographs, deer antlers and other ephemera placed alongside modern works by local artists. Food is served but not to the detriment of drinkers, though there might be a separate dining area. Bar snacks will be robust and unpretentious: expect homemade pies, real chips, granary rolls with ham and cheese and thick nourishing soups made from local produce.

TRY: the **Bow Bar** and **Thomson's**, both in Edinburgh; **Woods**, Dulverton, Somerset.

RURAL OUTPOST

A Labrador lies by the fire, barely moving his head as you creak open the door. In the winter the crackling of logs contends with the low hum of conversation as both regulars and visitors review the day's events. The summer sees all but the most cold-blooded move to the garden for a chance of supping in the sunlight. The licensee is affable and usually from the area: tap him or her for local knowledge about where best to roam or find a room for the night. The interior may be divided into several rooms, each as comfortable as the other. Pictures of folk from long ago, local events, maps and newspaper cuttings jostle for space on the walls. These are places where conversation is king, the beer is local and often drawn straight from the barrel, while the menu supports the farm down the road. Darts, skittles, quoits and the Sunday-night quiz keep people on their toes.

Try: the **King's Head** (Low House), Laxfield, Suffolk; the **Duke of York**, Iddesleigh, Devon.

MODERN MAKE-OVER

Regulars used to sit around and grumble about the price of a pint in this old-style boozer until a smart, youngish company with a penchant for beer took it over. Out went the dismal furnishings, the poorly pulled pints, the 'mockney' lager and indifferent food, and in came a new world of interesting beers from home and abroad, cosmopolitan food plus a young staff with a contagious enthusiasm for what they serve. Respect for the pub means that it still looks like somewhere to enjoy a drink. Lots of light, modern design and a positive vibe convert all but the most cantankerous, while cosy armchairs and sofas give a new meaning to comfort drinking. Here be raspberry beers alongside cask ales as well as American IPAs, organic beers and the odd lambic; sometimes there's a small brewery in situ or just around the corner. It's premium fare and you pay a price for your ale, but introducing a Belgian Pale Ale in its own glass to a visiting friend or surprising your mum with a kriek and a plate of salted almonds is well worth the price.

Try: the **Greenwich Union**, London; the **Duke of Cambridge**, Islington, London; the **Queen's Arms**, Corton Denham, Somerset.

The 10 essentials of a good pub

(according to Geoff Brandwood, co-author of *Licensed To Sell*, and a lifelong pub and beer enthusiast)

What makes a good pub...

1 The publican. Beyond all else it's the publican that counts. His/her attitude determines the customers who come and the whole atmosphere of the pub; he/she controls or, in the case of tied houses, influences the drinks on offer. Almost everything is down to the publican, including the role of food, the state of the loos, and the factors listed below.

2 Beer. Not much to say here. If the beer's no good, you go elsewhere!

3 Atmosphere. For the most part, good pubs are important social centres within their communities, but should be welcoming to strangers.

4 Food. Contrary to what you sometimes hear, food has for centuries been a part of what many pubs offer. So, decent homemade food please without the smell of cooking fat wafting into the bar.

5 Multi-rooms. I do like the idea of the traditional, multi-room pub. Different groups – young, old, pub game players, diners, and people at community meetings – can all have separate spaces with different atmospheres and facilities for their needs.

6 Smoking. No smoking or a separate room with first-rate extraction please.

7 Outdoor drinking. It's great to have a nice garden for an outdoor pint in good weather.

8 Kids. I'm all for parents being able to introduce their offspring to the world of the pub so long as there are separate facilities that do not impinge upon serious-minded drinkers like me!

9 Music. No. The pub is a place for conversation. Please don't invade my ears with music I didn't choose and don't want to listen to. And I don't need flashy machines either to gamble my drinking money away.

10 A sense of history. Pubs are part of our centuries-old heritage and to drink in one of CAMRA's National or Regional Inventory pubs – those with a good deal of genuinely historic planning and/or fittings – is always a pleasure. But spare us mock heritage, such as acres of imported pictures that have no connection with the local area, and unfounded tales of being ye oldest pub or that Dick Turpin drank there!

What spoils a pub...

1 Great big screen(s) for sports programmes.

2 More screens showing disconnected images with no sound.

3 Deafening music (often accompanied by the silent screens just mentioned!).

4 Café-style fittings and a brand new ambience (with 'women-friendly' plain glass windows).

5 Pubs targeting 'yoof' (especially on Friday and Saturday nights).

6 Barrages of obtrusive, often brightly lit, keg founts on the counter that form an obstacle course between customers and staff.

7 Massive structures standing on the counter for glasses, bottles and other kit.

8 Carpets in areas with likely spillage and where they serve as an oversized ashtray.

9 Smelly loos.

10 And last, but certainly not least, no real ale.

Relax and enjoy the traditions of an old country pub with a pint of local ale, or sample the global beers on offer in a modern city pub.

THE EXPORT OF THE PUB

THE PUB: A MOVABLE FEAST

The great British institution of the pub has travelled the globe and whether you're in Tenerife or Tokyo, chances are that you'll find an establishment loosely based on the British pub. Sometimes cask beers are for sale and the fittings can inspire a feeling homesickness among expatriates. On the other hand, the 'foreign British pub' is also notorious for being the last stronghold of anonymous keg beers with jingoistic names such as John Bull, as well as for serving the worst of British fare. This duplication may act as a tourist trap in some places, attracting those who have little interest in local culture, but it is also a real indicator of the enduring strength of the British pub-drinking tradition. As they say, imitation is the best form of flattery.

New World, new thinking – the American brewpub
Expect bright and modern airy spaces run by folk who pay as much attention to good cuisine as to excellent ale. Just as some restaurants have their chefs on display in the kitchen, so many American brewpubs allow customers the chance to keep an eye on the gleaming coppers and fermenting vessels that produce their beers. Samples in small glasses are common, which means that you can try an ESB, Baltic porter, oatmeal stout or American wheat beer over lunch. Have a nice day.

TRY: **Deschutes Brewery Brewpub**,
1044 NW Bond Street, Bend, Oregon.

Beer menu sir – drinking in a Brussels café bar
It's a bar Jim, but not as we know it. Ask for a beer and you'll be handed a menu listing up to 100 beers, some in cobwebbed bottles hidden in the cellar and others fresh and young from the tap. At the lower end of the

alcoholic scale there are faros, lambics and witbiers, while as the evening draws on those with a sense of adventure (or misadventure given the mind-numbing strength of some of the beers) are drawn to Trappist ales brewed by monks or Saison specialities brought to life on farms high up in the Ardennes. Wine-sized bottles are common so do share with a friend. All the beers are served in their own engraved and graciously

Whether in downtown America, the cobbled streets of Dublin or the Czech Republic, seek out the authentic pubs and bars that offer real ales and a unique atmosphere.

shaped glasses, and it's not unknown for the person behind the bar to refuse to serve a beer if there is not a suitable glass available. Bar staff are also knowledgable. Ask about a certain beer style and you will invariably get the history, chapter and verse. They take their beer seriously in this sort of establishment. As for food, some stick with light snacks, while others proffer a plateful of frites and moules, the beer-drinker's best pal to a glass of wit. The more adventurous try Toast Cannibale, which is a mixture of raw minced beef, gherkins, shallots and Tabasco amongst other things.

Try: the **Bier Circus**, 89 rue de l'Enseignement, Brussels; **Excelsoir**, 29 Grand' Place, Mons.

Bohemian rhapsody – on the beer in Prague
Local lads in suits, who in England would be knocking back Arctic-cool lagers, sup Pilsner Urquell with relish while polishing off a plate of pork knuckle.Others pick at snacks which are handed out with the beer: smoked cheese, cold meat, pickles and a soft, sweet mustard. The pub is bright and starkly lit: full of

businessmen, young and old, casuals, working men, couples and tourists. The food is filling; dumplings with lots of meat, so drop the diet and go with the flow. Pilsner Urquell is the main beer here, though Kozel Dark, a weak sweetish dark beer tasting not unlike the venerable sweet stout Mackeson, is worth a try. Staropramen and Budweiser Budvar are also popular.

Try: **U Pinkasu**, Jungmannovo namesti 15, Prague.

The spread of the Irish
It's St Patrick's night in Prague and time for a drink. How about Molly Malone's in the Old Town where homesick Irish men and women can guzzle Guinness, eat Irish Stew and listen to the music of their homeland being played by local musicians. Or maybe you're after some *craic* in the north Devon town of Bideford, the centre of Paris or even in the Columbian capital of Bogota. The Irish pub has taken over the world.

Indeed the Irish pub is an enduring classic. Whether it features a band of musicians playing away in the corner or a landlord who nips over to serve stout in an establishment that also doubles as a grocer's shop, the pub is often the first thing on most people's list to visit when in Ireland. Dublin has a great tradition of pubs from the grand Temple Bar to cosy McDaid.'s where the poet Brendan Behan was a regular.

In the 1990s, bright advertising whizzkids had the idea of transplanting what they thought was the authenticity of Irish pub culture. At the same time, fake 'Oirish' beers were being peddled, first of all in Britain, and then throughout Europe – which is why you will be served something called Kilkenny Cream Ale in the Old Square Irish Pub in Cagliari on the island of Sardinia. The pubs usually adopted names such as Scruffy Murphy's and O'Neill's, and featured all sorts of Irish-themed bric-a-brac (signposts from rural Ireland and bicycles anyone?) and genuine Irish music. Guinness of course was omnipresent.

Irish-themed pubs are all based on an advertising gimmick, but pubs where the peripatetic Irish gather, wherever they travel, are the real thing, as anyone who has visited one in Boston, New York or London can testify... and not a signpost in sight.

Try: **Temple Bar**, Temple Bar, Dublin; **Porterhouse**, Parliament Streeet, Dublin; **McDaids**, Harry Street, Dublin

PUB GAMES

The British pub is home to a whole host of games, some of which have their roots firmly embedded in the Merrie England tradition of maypoles, church ales and licensed tomfoolery. In comparison, darts and pools are positive upstarts. Darts has been traced back to 19th-century fairgrounds where blowpipes were used; dominoes came over from Italy in the days of Queen Victoria, while pool arrived as recently as the 1960s from America. On the other hand, games such as skittles, Aunt Sally, shove ha'penny, quoits and bat and trap have entertained the pub-going yeomanry of the British Isles for centuries. Aunt Sally, a form of skittles that involves throwing sticks at a skittle on a post, reputedly has its origins in the English Civil Wars. Quoits avows an even more venerable past. Some aficionados claim that quoits is nothing less than an Anglicised version of discus-throwing, and insist the game's ancestry can be traced back to Ancient Greece. Skittles can't claim such classical origins but still has a highly respectable family-tree dating back to the Middle Ages. The game has several different variations around the country including Hood Skittles and Devil Among The Tailors.

The pub is also home to a variety of team games, which may not have the history and heritage of the ones already mentioned but they are still an integral part of the pub. What would this venerable institution be like without the darts team's regular battles with neighbouring pubs. Or the French games of pentanque and boules which have drawn many pub-goers into their ranks. And let us not forget the myriads pub quizzes up and down Britain, where pub teams congregate to test their wits against each other.

WHAT TO PLAY AND WHERE TO PLAY IT

Aunt Sally throwing a stick at a wooden skittle called a doll – Oxfordshire

Quoits throwing steel rings at a pin stuck in a clay pit – north-east England, Scotland and Wales

Ringing The Bull pitching a metal ring that dangles on a rope from the ceiling onto a metal hook on the wall – mainly northern England

Skittles knock over nine pins, including 'the landlord' (the largest) with a large wooden ball – West Country; the Long Alley version, which is played with a hardwood 'cheese' is found in the East Midlands; while Hood Skittles, also involving a 'cheese', is found in Northampton

Devil Among The Tailors a table version of skittles – mainly northern England

Bat and Trap from the same family as cricket; this involves hitting a ball after it has sprung out of a trap – mainly Kent

The table skittles game Devil Among the Tailors can still be found in some northern pubs (main picture), while many pub-goers still enjoy playing games of dominoes and pool.

BEER TO STAY HOME FOR

BEER TO GO BACK WITH

You want a beer, but can't be bothered to go down the pub? Shame on you. Or maybe you've got some mates coming round for a pizza and you want to give them real beer. There's a barbecue, a picnic, a celebration, and you feel the urge to avoid the wine trail. You're a couch potato and fancy drinking real beer with flavour, depth and character without shifting from your sofa. What to do? The more intrepid have been known to go down the pub with a four-pint plastic jug and buy beer straight from the bar, thus carrying on the ancient jug and bottle tradition. Some breweries, especially in the UK, offer beer in a plastic polypin, a cask-conditioned beer complete with yeast working away. These can either be bought straight from the brewery or delivered to your home (be warned, beer is heavy so postage is expensive).

However, there are drawbacks to buying beer in bulk. Beer boxes sometimes contain a minimum of 18 pints, which is a lot to get through in a weekend if you live alone and don't want the neighbours talking. Beer poured from a plastic jug a couple of hours after it has come from the tap has lost some (if not all) of its conditioning. There is one other option, though. Step forward, bottle-conditioned beer, living beers that have been bottled with a yeast sediment so they continue maturing in the bottle.

Beer from the cask

When real beer is racked into cask, it still has to spend some time maturing at the brewery and in the pub cellar before it is ready to be drunk. In this time, the yeast in the cask helps to generate a secondary fermentation. If you order a cask of your favourite beer from a brewery for a celebration, it may have been 'dropped bright', which means that the yeast has been filtered out and the beer is ready to drink as soon as the cask is set up. Other times, you will have to wait for up to a day before the beer clears. The cask should be stored horizontally to enable the finings to clarify the beer.

Next job is to tap and vent the cask, a process of drawing off some of the carbon dioxide that has been produced by the secondary fermentation. Temperature is also important at this stage. Pub cellars should be kept at about 11°C (52°F), though some brewers are now serving their beers slightly cooler, especially in pubs where there is a young clientele who are used to the mouth-numbingly cold temperatures of some lagers. At home, keep your cask in a cool space: fluctuations in temperature can ruin a good beer.

Live beer can be a tempestuous creature and should be treated as if it were a fine wine. Some breweries produce their beers in a box, complete with yeast working away. Again, the rule of thumb is to keep it cool and not to shake it about. Treat your beer with reverence and it will reward you with plenty of flavour and aroma.

BOTTLE-CONDITIONED BEERS

Once upon a time most bottled beers would have been bottle-conditioned, but the rise of clear glassware in the latter decades of the19th century led to a demand for beer without yeast in it (if shaken, the beer would become cloudy and take some time to clear again, which was a big minus if you wanted a drink now rather than later). Meanwhile the development of pasteurisation showed that beers could be filtered and pasteurised in the bottle without harming the flavour. Added carbon dioxide gave them sparkle, and they were also deemed to be easier to pour as you didn't have to worry about great clumps of yeast cluttering up your glass.

In the 1970s, there were only five bottle-conditioned beers available in the UK: Guinness Extra Stout, Courage's Russian Imperial Stout, Gale's Prize Old Ale, Worthington's White Shield and Thomas Hardy's Ale (other beer nations such as Belgium and Germany had a few more including Trappist beers and Bavarian Weisse). The last three are still around, but have been joined by hundreds of other beers from both regional and microbreweries. Some, such as Hop Back's Summer Lightning, Fuller's 1845 and Young's Special London Ale are available through supermarkets and off-licences (along with their European and American cousins such as Westmalle's Dubbel, Hoegaarden and Sierra Nevada Pale Ale). Many of the smaller brewers sell their beers through specialist beer shops, online or at the brewery gate. There are also competitions such as the annual Champion Bottle-Conditioned Beer of Great Britain held at the annual Great British Beer Festival, each August.

As for production, some brewers bottle straight from cask, though the quality for this mode of production can be very hit and miss. Others filter out old yeast and add fresh yeast, while some 'kräusen' their beer – they add partially fermented wort to give the yeast more fermentable sugars to snack on. The best are beers that continue to mature in the bottle, developing more rounded and deeper flavours. When a bottle-conditioned beer is on form you have a superb live beer that can serve not only as an interesting aperitif but also has intriguing possibilities as an alternative to wine with the meal. It is also something to tantalise those drinkers who think that wine and whisky are the only drinks that improve with time.

CREATING YOUR OWN BEER CELLAR

People put wine on a pedestal, but knock down beer. There are wine snobs but beer bores. When children are born, christened or come of age, cases of wine are laid down for them; beer on the other hand is thought fit only for the party, to be bought in bulk and as cheaply as possible. People buy wine as an investment, but beer is seen as being for the here and now, which is true for a lot of beautifully crafted everyday drinking beers – but some beers do have a longer lifeline.

BEER FOR KEEPING

A growing band of brewers are giving us beers for the future; beers to lay down and mature over the coming years. These are beers that demand the treatment of fine wines. The bottles must be stored in cool dark places away from sunlight and extremes of temperature. Many are bottle-conditioned with the yeast still working its magic as secondary fermentation takes place, subtly changing the beer's personality. These are also beers that are strong and therefore need to be treated with reverence. Over the years, the taste of a vintage beer changes and develops: hoppiness gets softer, maltiness more rounded and the complexity of the beer increases.

Brewing beer to last used to be a matter of necessity rather than choice. Before brewing became totally industrialised, and brewers and chemists uncovered the mysteries of yeast, brewing was a seasonal activity. Because high summer temperatures rendered brewing difficult during that period, beers in the spring would be made very strong – the alcohol would keep the beers free from contamination during the summer and there would be something to quaff as the leaves fell. In Victorian times, brewers also made very strong Stock Ales (in the autumn), which after maturation in the cask would be blended with weaker ales. Suffolk brewers Greene King continue this tradition: a well-matured beer called Old 5X (12%) is mixed in with a younger, fresher and less alcoholic ale BPA (5%). This is then released as the excellent Strong Suffolk Vintage Ale (6%).

One of the most legendary long-lasting vintage beers was Thomas Hardy's Ale (12%), formerly from Eldridge Pope in Dorchester. This was a masterly ale, first brewed in 1968, and coming with the recommendation that it would be drinkable for 25 years. Ageing Thomas Hardys are known to develop flavours such as figs, dates, currants, treacle, caramel, and chocolate. The 1999 vintage was the last one brewed by the Thomas Hardy brewery (as Eldridge Pope was then called), who decided brewing such a specialist beer in small numbers was uneconomical. Now O'Hanlon's in Devon have taken on the commission to brew Thomas Hardy's Ale again. So far there have been two breathtakingly wonderful vintages.

Fuller's of West London have also found a gap in the fine ale market with their bottle-conditioned Vintage Ale (8.5%), which appears every year. 'Our first Vintage Ale was in 1997,' says Fuller's Brewing Director John Keeling. 'We spent two years prior to that thinking about a beer which would use the best raw materials. We also wanted a beer that would generate interest in our beers and decided to make it a limited edition. Finally we wanted it to mature and change its flavour over time. It was a case of if you waited over a period of time it would change flavours. I am surprised over the amount of people who bought up lots of 1997's vintage to compare it over time. It would be interesting to see how it lasts.'

> **Beer is served**
>
> Pour the bottle with care and it won't be cloudy. Keep it cool and the flavour will be ripe and tempting. Enjoy

White Shield

Twenty years ago, bottle-conditioned Worthington White Shield was an ideal stand-by if you went into a cask-ale-free pub, as it was the only real ale in a bottle which was stocked by pubs. It was brewed in Burton-on-Trent and as close to an old-style Pale Ale as you could get. Bar staff prided themselves on being able to pour the beer into a glass without letting in any of the yeast, which gave the beer such complexity. The theatre to this style of service helped the image of the beer. The beer was also pretty delicious with an excellent balance of malt sweetness and fruity hop on the palate followed by a long bitter finish. After being brewed in several locations, White Shield is back in Burton, under the control of Steve Wellington of the White Shield Brewery (formerly called Museum), at the old Bass headquarters, now owned by American corporate giants Coors.

Beers such as Fuller's Vintage Ale, Samuel Adams Triple Bock and Rochefort 10 are the beery equivalents of the Chateaux Lafittes and Talbots of wine. Like good wines, good beers improve with time. It's not just dark beers that can be stored either. IPAs were brewed in the 19th century to last the long journey to India so it makes sense to lay down true IPAs made by the likes of Burton Bridge, Pitfield and Freeminer. Other beers desperate for a rest in the dark include Woodforde's Norfolk's Nips and Headcracker, Cottage's Norman's Conquest, Old Freddy Walker, Durham Brewery's Benedictus and Worthington White Shield. Looking abroad, there are daringly hopped strong IPAs from America (Dogfish Head 90 Minute IPA, Rogue Imperial India Pale Ale), Sri Lankan stouts from Lion Brewery, Austrian strong lagers from Eggenberg and Belgian Trappist beers (including the aforementioned Rochefort) which are also necessities for the well-stocked beer cellar. A few non-bottle-conditioned beers will keep as well. These are usually very strong in alcohol (which helps with preservation) and include the likes of the 14% kaiser of a lager Samichlaus, Lees Harvest Ale and strong beers from American microbreweries.

STORING BEER

How beer is stored affects its condition. Keep beers in a cool temperature, away from extremes of heat (consistency is all), strong smells and direct sunlight, which can dry out corks, bleach the labels and speed up the ageing of the beer. Do not keep the bottles in the kitchen. If beer is in clear bottles, the action of light may cause 'skunking', which produces off-flavours. Beer exposed to warmth can be pasteurised and then the great complexities of flavour are lost. Beers with corks in them should be laid on their side to avoid cork leakage letting in oxygen. Those with metal crown caps should be stored upright. Bottle-conditioned beers should be kept still for at least 24 hours before serving and should never be shaken.

Finally, depending on how many bottles you are storing you may want to organise them by style and strength. Put the ones that are in for the long haul at the back, while the ones you want to drink soon go to the front.

Cupboard love – beers to keep

Note: not B/C means not bottle-conditioned

BEERS TO DRINK NOW OR KEEP FOR SIX MONTHS
Adnams Broadside (not B/C)
Breconshire Golden Valley
Coors Worthington's White Shield
Coopers Sparkling Ale (Australia)
Cottage Norman's Conquest
Goose Island India Pale Ale (USA)
Achouffe La Chouffe (Belgium)
Marston's Old Empire (not B/C)
O'Hanlon's Port Stout
RCH East Street Cream (not B/C)
St Austell Clouded Yellow
Woodforde's Headcracker
Wye Valley Dorothy Goodbody's Wholesome Stout

BEERS TO KEEP FOR A YEAR
Alaskan Smoked Porter (USA)
Burton Bridge Empire Ale
Burton Bridge Tickle Brain
Coors P2
Coors No1 Barley Wine
Eggenberg Urbock (Austria, not B/C)
Brasserie Saint Sylvestre Gavroche (France)
La Trappe Quadrupel (Holland)
Moor Brewing Company Old Freddy Walker
Orkney Skullsplitter (not B/C)
Parish Baz's Bonce Blower
Pitfield 1792 Imperial Stout
Rogue Imperial Stout (USA, not B/C)
Schneider Aventinus (Germany)
Sierra Nevada Bigfoot Barley Wine (USA)
Teignworthy Edwin Tucker's East India Pale Ale
Westmalle Tripel (Belgium)
Woodforde's Norfolk Nip
Victory Golden Monkey Tripel Ale (USA)

BEERS TO KEEP FOR TWO YEARS OR MORE
Anchor Old Foghorn Barley Wine (USA, not B/C)
Brooklyn Brewery Black Chocolate Stout (USA, not B/C)
Dogfish Head Worldwide Stout (USA, not B/C)
Eggenberg Samischlaus (Austria, not B/C)
Fuller's Vintage Ale
Gale's Prize Old Ale
Harveys Imperial Extra Double Stout
La Chouffe N'ice (Belgium)
Lees Harvest Ale (not B/C)
Pitfield 1896 XXXX Stock Ale
Thomas Hardy's Ale
Teignworthy Edwin Tucker's Empress Russian Porter
Westvleteren 12 (Belgium)

KEEPING A CELLAR BOOK

There are many styles of cellar books for wine but none for beer, so you'll need to improvise. Take a standard wine cellar book and adapt it for your own use. You should list the country of origin, the brewer, how many bottles, where stored, the type or style, name and strength, the year if mentioned, where and when it was purchased and the price. When you come to drink the beer, note the date and your thoughts on what you have drunk. Also make a note of how many (if any) of this particular beer you have left. This book will be a definitive record of some of the great beers you have enjoyed through the years.

HOW LONG TO CHILL A BEER?

Most beers, and certainly all lagers, need to spend a certain time in the cool of your fridge. The idea of warm beer is a myth. For ales, porters and stouts allow half an hour to an hour unless you have kept the beer overnight in a cool room. If beer is too cold, allow it to warm up in the glass to release its enticing aromas. If it's too warm, you're stuck, as short of adding a few ice cubes there's nothing you can do. Czech and German lagers require a few hours to cool. Wheat beers and fruit beers also benefit from a certain chill. But don't be tempted to cheat by putting bottles in the ice box.

SERVING BOTTLED BEER

Pouring beer from a bottle is a straightforward activity. Hold the glass nearly horizontal and start dribbling the beer in, letting the glass get more vertical as the bottle empties. This avoids the excess of foam that results from letting the beer crash down into the glass from a height. If there is yeast in the bottle, let it stay in the shoulder. However, for a German wheat beer or Belgian witbier the yeast is part of the drink and is usually swirled in at the end. Don't be scared, there are valuable minerals and vitamins here.

BEER PEOPLE

Gary Marshall, Landlord

BLISLAND INN, *Blisland, Cornwall*

'The interest in real ales was a gradual thing. I suppose it started at the start of the 1990s. I was still in the Navy but helped out at a pub in Plymouth. It was a Courage pub, and I liked it. People come here for beer and we support all the local brewers. We have had Cornish beer festivals, and we often do a theme for a month. What makes a successful pub is a hands-on attitude with a good personal service. People want traditional beer and food and a good atmosphere. Here the lager's tucked away and there's no nitrokeg.

I always talk people into trying a different beer. I'm keen on pushing new beers on people. You name it, we've had it: chocolate beers, honey beers such as Skinner's Heligan Honey which is excellent. It all gets people interested in beer and I find both men and women trying it. Because we're a specialist cask beer pub, people come here to drink cask beer, there's always something on each month. Cherry Bomb from Hanby is excellent for instance. Some may think it's gimmicky but they are usually the traditional bitter drinkers in the corner who haven't changed their beer for years.'

John Sumbland, Landlord

THE PENRHYN ARMS, *Penrhynside, near Llandudno, North Wales*

'I had my first taste of real ale when I was 16. I'd gone to a wedding in Bolton and went to the pub with my uncles. They bought me a pint of cask Chester's Mild and I loved it. I was hooked. When we moved to Wales, none of the pubs sold cask mild so I went on to bitter.

When we took over this pub in 2003, real beer was the way I wanted to take it. People told me there was no money in it, that there was too much waste, yet I knew that people would travel for good real ale. I also wanted to introduce people to different beers. Most people had drunk the likes of Old Speckled Hen, Abbot and the others you tend to see in pubs, so I spent time looking for different beers. I love it when I look down the bar and see a load of people drinking real ale. It creates a lot of interest when I put the Beer Menu for the coming month on the bar. When my costumers go away for a holiday in the UK, the postcards I get don't have the usual stuff written on the back about the weather or the hotel. Instead, they will tell me what real ales they've had and some times they come back with the name and address of the brewery, plus a contact name.

First and foremost, the essence of a good pub is the welcome when you come in. And people who serve you know what they are selling, especially with the real ale. When you ask what a beer is like, you don't want to hear: 'I haven't a clue. I only drink lager or Bud.' I only have one barmaid beside my wife Sharon, and I tell her what the beers are like so she can tell customers.

I think you have to enjoy being behind the bar. It's hard work and long hours but I love it. I'm a failed stand-up comedian and a bar-room poet, so I have a captive audience that gives me money.'

BEER AND FOOD

Whether it's a long cool glass of
wheat beer with fish and chips,
a glass of GUEUZE with pickled herring or a
nip of BARLEY WINE with a wedge of Stilton,
BEER AND FOOD make great
companions at the dinner table.

BEER IS THE NEW WINE

BEER IS SERVED

Beer and food in Britain used to mean a pint and sandwich or the landlord's 'special' steak and Guinness pie, its arrival heralded by the ping of a microwave oven. Beer was just about tolerated served with seafood, especially Guinness, while canny cooks added beer to their batter to help it rise to the occasion (though fizzy lemonade is just as good). But for the most part, 'beer cuisine' (cooking with beer and teaming beer to drink with food) was an alien notion. Prevailing wisdom declared that wine was the ideal companion to food. As a result of this prejudice, very few drinkers or diners knew of the pleasures of a barley wine alongside a ripe wedge of Stilton, or the champagne-like spritzy treat of a wheat beer served with fish and chips. Even fewer would have guessed that this parlous state of affairs had not always been the case. In the Victorian age, no dining table was complete without a bottle (or three) of beer, whether it was a sparkling golden India Pale Ale or a thirst-quenching Dinner Ale or Luncheon Stout. Meanwhile, Pickwick Club types could fortify themselves at the table with flagons of foaming porter, while strong Audit Ales were passed around with the port at the end of Oxbridge college dinners.

However, the 20th century saw wine don its cloak of respectability as the middle classes sought to put a greater distance between themselves and those whom they saw as their beer-drinking inferiors (an intriguing by-product of this culinary snobbery was the brief emergence of perry at the table for less well-off families). The new century brings new attitudes. Pioneering brewers, chefs and publicans are sneaking beer back onto the table and finding that John Barleycorn is a perfect partner for everything from hearty French cuisine to spicy New World innovations. All that sparkles in a wine glass is not necessarily the perfect guest at the table. Spicy food warps the character of red wine, adding an extra and unnecessary level of heat. Beer, however, is refreshing and its carbonation can help to clear the palate, something only champagne in the wine family can do. Some beers have roast and caramelised flavours and aromas, which are notably missing in wine. Wine buffs readily agree that their favoured beverage has a problem with certain foods. Why bother to match a chocolate dessert with wine when a chocolate or fruit beer can do the business with style? This is not meant to belittle wine, but to show that the grape doesn't have all the answers. It is said that matching wine and food is about contrast and colour, while beer and food is about harmony as well as contrast.

MATCHING BEER AND FOOD

Beer and food are natural companions at the table. The malty sweetness that appears in beer picks out the parallel sweetness in a meat such as pork, or it can match the sweet-fruitiness of desserts. Roast malts give beer smoky and roast features: step forward roast meat and barbecues. As for fish, think of the sweetness that malt gives to the background of beer, but go easy on the hops as the delicate flesh can be overwhelmed; fresh and flowery Pilsners and English-style wheat beers are piscatorial favourites. Then there are hops, beer's noble equivalent to grapes. Spicy, peppery aftertastes from some chime well

*Matching beer and
food is about harmony
as well as contrast.*

with spicy food, while citrus and orange marmalade
notes on others make an interesting friend to cheese
and pickles. The bitterness from hops also cuts
through fatty foods and leaves the palate clean and
refreshed for the next mouthful. Try a big-flavoured,
hop-happy American IPA with cassoulet and see
how the action of the hop bitterness and refreshing
carbonation cleans the palate for another mouthful.
Experience the herby, perfumy, earthy flavours of
a French bière de garde with roast lamb and mint.
Or take it easy and sip a London chocolate stout
alongside a chocolate dessert. Harmony, harmony,
harmony. In Europe and the America it's neither
new nor particularly revolutionary. Visit Prague
and a Pilsner Urquell or Budweiser Budvar will be
the only thing to serve with a dish of dumplings and
pork, or you can search out a beer cheese which is
exactly what its name describes. In Bavaria, pork
knuckle and plenty on the side comes with a wheat
beer or a dark and delicious Dunkel or Doppel Bock.
American brewpubs have always been ahead of the
game as they pair up their adventurous beer styles
with food and splash it about in the kitchen. Yet in
Britain, despite the titanic efforts of many brewers
and beer writers, beer's social standing still remains
low. Become a beer ambassador yourself; try sampling
different beers with your food and note how they
work together. Next time you go to a dinner party or
picnic, try taking along a few well-selected bottles
for friends to sample. Mix and match the flavours
in food and beer and break free from the prevailing
thought that only wine will do at the dinner table.

BEER AS A CULINARY INGREDIENT

Pairing beer and food is about matching flavour with flavour, while beer as an ingredient in the kitchen can tease out the flavours of a particular dish. Braise root vegetables with a porter to bring out their inherent sweetness. How about cheese and ale soup, ale bread and German sausage steamed in stout or Scottish Ale served with a pork roast?

Now all this has been catching on in the UK. There are beer menus, beers to dine for, real beer and real food. British breweries such as Greene King, Hook Norton, Caledonian, St Austell and Fuller's let beer-lovers know which meals best accompany their fine ales. How about homemade sausages marinaded in Dorset brewers Badger's strong ale Tanglefoot, and a sticky ginger cake best served with their Blandford Fly ginger-tinged bitter? Suffolk brewers Greene King went one step further and teamed up with London restaurateur Michael Moore to produce a beer menu on which Strong Suffolk was served with oysters, Abbot Ale with duck in hoisin sauce and Ruddles County with smoked salmon. Smaller British brewers have also joined in: O'Hanlon's of Devon include food and beer pairings on the labels of their excellent bottle-conditioned beers, while Oakham Ales suggest their award-winning JHB with the spicy Thai dishes that they serve up at their Birmingham pub, the Bartons Arms.

In the kitchen and on the dining table, beer has grown up: it's jostling for space with wine and has every right to be seen as more than just a pint of Best.

Ginger up pudding time with a drop of Badger's spicy Blandford Fly.

SAMPLE OUR SELECTION OF
FINE REAL ALES FROM AWARD WINNING
BREWERIES, INCLUDING

- ADNAM'S EXTRA FROM SOUTHWOLD
  IN SUFFOLK
- HARVEY'S BEST BITTER FROM LEWES,
  EAST SUSSEX
- HIGHGATE DARK MILD
  IN TH

RECIPES WITH BEER

Kedgeree with India Pale Ale

(SERVES 4–6)

This recipe, based on an imperial breakfast favourite, is from *The Beer Cook Book* by Susan Nowak, courtesy of the author.

550g (1lb 4 oz) naturally smoked haddock

300ml (10 fl oz) IPA such as Marston's Old Empire, Freeminer's Trafalgar or Goose Island IPA

1 bay leaf

2 sprigs fresh parsley

3 peppercorns

3–4 saffron strands

2 rashers smoked streaky bacon, de-rinded and sliced

50g (2oz) unsalted butter

1 small red onion, diced

2 cloves garlic, crushed

1 stick celery, sliced finely

1 tsp cumin

2 tsp garam masala

½ tsp powdered ginger

225g (8oz) Basmati rice, rinsed, soaked and drained

3 cardamons

12 quails eggs, hardboiled and shelled

100g (4oz) cooked shell-on prawns

3 tbsp fresh coriander, chopped

1 fresh lemon cut into wedges

Method

Place the haddock in a single layer in a large frying pan. Pour over the IPA and add the bay leaf, fresh parsley and peppercorns. Cover and simmer gently for 5 minutes, then leave to cool. ¶ Remove the fish and flake it into large chunks, discarding the skin and bones. Strain the beer liquor into a measuring jug, add the saffron strands and make up to 300 ml (10 fl oz) with hot water, if necessary. ¶ In a heavy-bottomed frying pan, sweat the bacon until the fat runs out. Add the butter and gently fry the onion, garlic and celery for 2 minutes without browning. Stir in the cumin, garam masala and ginger and continue to fry gently, stirring, for another minute. Add the drained rice and stir gently to coat the grains with spiced butter. Add cardamons and strain on the liquor. Stir once and cover, then simmer on a low heat for 5 minutes. Take off the heat and leave to stand for another 5 minutes until the rice is tender and virtually all the stock is absorbed. ¶ Meanwhile shell 9 of the hard-boiled quails' eggs and halve lengthways. Shell all but 3 of the prawns and cut in half. Gently fork the smoked haddock chunks into the rice over a low heat, followed by the halved eggs, shelled prawns and fresh coriander. ¶ Pile on to a large warm serving plate, decorating the top with the remaining quails' eggs and prawns still in their shells, and place lemon wedges round the dish.

DRINK: **English or American IPA**

Beef Carbonnade in Old Freddy Walker

(SERVES 4)

This variation on the classic Flemish stew uses strong dark ale Old Freddy Walker (7.3%) from South Wales-based brewery Moor. Also try Young's Old Nick (7.2%) or Norfolk Nips (8.5%) from Woodforde.

1.4 kg (1lb 8oz) braising beef, cubed

300ml (10 fl oz) Old Freddy Walker

bay leaf

a few mixed peppercorns

bouquet garni

salt and pepper to season

1 Spanish onion, sliced

1 clove garlic, chopped

1 tbsp plain flour

1 leek, sliced

1 swede, diced into chunks

2 small carrots, diced into chunks

olive oil

toasted sesame oil

pinch of brown sugar

fresh marjoram

300ml (10 fl oz) beef stock

white vine vinegar

Method

Marinade the beef in Old Freddy Walker overnight with bay leaf, peppercorns and bouquet garni. ¶ Next day, gently fry the onion and garlic in a dash of olive oil, then add the leek, swede and carrots. Cook until the onions are soft. Preheat the oven to 300°F, 150°C, gas mark 2. ¶ Meanwhile take the beef out of the marinade and pat it dry. Then brown the meat in a dash of toasted sesame oil; this gives a delectable hint of smokiness to the stew. ¶ Put the vegetables in a large casserole dish, add the meat and mix in a spoonful of plain flour. Season with salt and pepper. Stir in the beer marinade and beef stock. Sprinkle in a pinch of sugar and chopped marjoram. Heat to simmer, then cover the casserole and place in the oven. Cook for 2–3 hours until the beef is tender. Stir in a dash of white wine vinegar at the end and reheat briefly if necessary. ¶ Serve with mashed potatoes, onion cakes and young turnips.

DRINK: **Old Freddy Walker**

Rabbit with Mustard and Fuller's 1845

(SERVES 6)

The countryside meets urban London in this gamey casserole from *The Beer Cook Book* by Susan Nowak, courtesy of the author.

1 wild rabbit

4 green peppercorns

200 ml (7 fl oz) Fuller's 1845

1 tbsp plain flour

1 tbsp mustard powder

1 small onion, diced

1 small leek, shredded

2 rashers smoked streaky bacon, chopped

duck fat for frying

1 stick celery, chopped

1 carrot, diced

50g (2oz) chestnut mushrooms

25g (1oz) dried ceps, soaked in warm water

200 ml (7 fl oz) water

1 tbsp thyme

grating of nutmeg

seasoning

Method

Marinate the jointed rabbit overnight with peppercorns and beer. ¶ Preheat the oven to 350°F, 180°C, gas mark 4. Mix the flour and mustard together on a plate and dust the dried rabbit pieces. ¶ Melt a little fat in a frying pan and fry the bacon for a minute, then add the onion and leek and cook gently until soft. Transfer to a casserole dish. ¶ Fry the rabbit portions in a pan with a little more fat until browned, then add to the casserole with celery, carrot, chestnut mushrooms, and the ceps with their soaking water. Pour over the beer marinade and the water; add the thyme and a pinch of nutmeg. Cook in the middle of the oven for around 3 hours, until the rabbit is tender. Season to taste. Serve with mashed potatoes and parsnips.

DRINK: **Fuller's 1845**

Coq à la bière (SERVES 6)

A Northern France beery twist on the old French wine classic from *The Beer Cook Book* by Susan Nowak, courtesy of the author.

100g (4oz) fresh chicken livers
50g (2oz) pale part of leek, shredded and chopped finely
butter for frying
4 fat cloves of garlic
100g (4oz) smoked back bacon (with some fat) cut into strips
24 shallots skinned
12 free-range chicken thighs, boned
50g (2oz) seasoned flour
100g (4oz) small button mushrooms
1 measure of brandy
300 ml (10 fl oz) bière de garde
1 tbsp light brown sugar
fresh sage leaves
salt and freshly ground pepper

Method

First make a very simple paté by sautéing the fresh livers gently in butter with the leek and 2 crushed garlic cloves in a covered frying pan. After a few minutes, when the livers are soft and cooked through, season with salt and pepper, then mash up the livers and leek in their juices and put in the fridge to firm up. ¶ In the same frying pan melt a little butter, then scatter in bacon strips, followed by the shallots and fry gently for a few minutes until browned and slightly caramelised. Remove the bacon and shallots with a slotted spoon and place in a flat-bottomed casserole. Take about 1 tsp of the 'paté', roll it into a small ball, and gently stuff into a chicken thigh, pulling the loose edges together so that the stuffing is enclosed. ¶ Heat the oven to 350°F, 180°C, gas mark 4. Coat each thigh in seasoned flour, taking care not to let the filling fall out. Brown on all sides in the bacon fat, again carefully. Warm the brandy gently, pour it over the chicken pieces, and flame. Place the chicken thighs, edges side down, among the onions in the casserole then deglaze the pan with a little of the beer, bringing it to the bubble. Remove the frying pan from the heat and stir in the rest of the bière de garde and sugar, then pour the mixture over the chicken. Tuck three sage leaves among the chicken pieces and distribute mushrooms in any gaps. Cover with foil or a lid and cook in the middle of the oven until the chicken is tender – about 90 minutes. ¶ Discard the sage leaves and arrange the chicken pieces, shallots, bacon and mushrooms on a large platter. Pour the stock into a pan, season to taste, then reduce by about a third; pour over the chicken pieces and serve.

DRINK: bière de garde such as **Jenlain** or **Cuvée des Jonquilles**

Mushroom, Dorset Blue Vinney and Champion Galette

(SERVES 4)

A crumbly open tart ideal for weekend lunches from a recipe by Badger Ales, Dorset.

25g (1oz) dried wild mushrooms such as porcini or chanterelles
100ml (4fl oz) Badger Golden Champion Ale
100ml (4fl oz) boiling water
75g (3oz) butter
275g (10oz) flaky pastry
200g (7oz) organic chestnut mushrooms, chopped
200g (7oz) fresh wild mushrooms, chopped
2 medium onions, thinly sliced
1 clove garlic, minced
Handful each of chopped fresh rosemary and thyme
125g (5oz) Dorset Blue Vinny, or similar blue cheese such as Shropshire Blue

Method

Heat the oven to 400°F, 200°C, gas mark 6. Place the dried mushrooms in small bowl, add the boiling water and Badger Golden Champion Ale. Stand for 30 minutes until softened, then drain the mushrooms and chop. ¶ Heat the butter in a large frying pan, add the onions and garlic and sauté for 5 minutes until soft. Add the rosemary and thyme and continue to cook. Turn the heat to high, add the fresh mushrooms and sauté until they release their juices, then add the dried mushrooms and the juices they were soaked in. Cook until most of the liquid has evaporated, then turn off the heat and cool. ¶ Roll out the pastry into a large circle and place on a baking sheet. Crumble Dorset Blue cheese into the cooled mushroom mixture, then pile the mixture into the middle of the pastry base, leaving a 5cm gap. Carefully pleat the pastry overlap around the mushroom mixture to create a 'wreath' with the mixture still exposed in the middle of the tart. Bake for 35–40 minutes. Serve piping hot.

DRINK: **Badger Golden Champion Ale**

Chocolate Stout and Hazelnut Parfait

(SERVES 6)

Pure indulgence for beer-loving choco-holics, this recipe was developed by Susan Nowak for the Campaign For Real Ale.

8 tbsp chocolate stout
450 ml (15 fl oz) double cream
40 g (1½oz) caster sugar
4 egg yolks
100 g (4oz) milk chocolate
50 g (2oz) chopped hazelnuts

Method

In a heavy pan, boil the stout to reduce by half, taking care not to let it boil over. Add the sugar and stir constantly with a wooden spoon until it has dissolved. Bring to the boil again and simmer briskly until you get a light syrup (2–4 minutes) then set aside to cool. ¶ In a mixing bowl, whisk egg yolks, then pour on the beer syrup, whisking continuously. Melt the chocolate in a small glass bowl over hot water, then whisk it into the beer syrup and egg mix, and leave it to cool. When cold, fold in the double cream gradually, then churn in an ice-cream machine (or pour into a plastic container and freeze, removing occasionally to stir as it sets) mixing in the chopped hazelnuts as it freezes. Serve two scoops per portion with thick clotted cream.

DRINK: **Young's Double Chocolate Stout**, **Meantime's Chocolate Beer** or **Brooklyn Brewery's Dark Chocolate Stout**

ON BEER AND FOOD

THE SLOW FOOD MOVEMENT

In a world where a fast food hamburger, made from the fat and gristle of several cows, was seen as a meal, there simply had to be a backlash. It came from Italy in 1986 in the guise of the Slow Food movement. Slow Food is about the enjoyment of real food, free from the one-size-fits-all homogenisation of burger bars and restaurant chains where the food is the same regardless of the city, or even the country, in which it is served. Slow Food promotes local gastronomic cultures and aims to protect these local and traditional treasures by alerting the world to their pleasures. It is neither haute cuisine nor low cuisine, but simply real cuisine.

So what does this have to do with beer? A lot. For a start, think about American craft beers, British cask ales, local Bavarian Weisse and Wallonian Trappist beers. These are all hand-crafted beers, with raw materials sourced from the best suppliers. Traditions are made relevant to the modern world without compromise and the result is belting beers with bags of character and flavour. These are the artisanal contrasts to 'fast food' brewing, where accountants rather than brewers rule the roost and beers taste the same wherever they are made throughout the world.

Slow Food (and drink) is also about time, taking the time to appreciate real food and real beer, sometimes together, sometimes separately. Think of the pub, the bar, or the café where the world can be watched with a glass in hand. It is also about seeking out and savouring local tastes and styles; a fragrant and fruity Kölsch in Cologne, a spritzy Sparkling Ale in Adelaide, a clean tasting black beer in Osaka or a cool pint of bitter bursting with hop aromas and malty

bite in an English country inn. Slow Food is the staunch enemy of international food and drink. It is also the cheerleader for arcane food and beer styles that run the risk of falling out of fickle fashion. Whether it's a non-pasteurised cheese made high up in the northern Italian mountains or a challenging and authentic lambic from the environs of Brussels, the Slow Food movement wants such minority tastes to survive. Like its kindred spirit, the organic movement, Slow Food is about pleasure and taking the time to enjoy that pleasure.

The Slow Food movement is about taking the time to produce authentic food and drink such as the Belgium speciality lambic, as shown here.

BEER MATCHMAKERS

Mark Dorber,
*landlord at the White Horse, Parsons Green,
and the Anchor, Walberswick, Suffolk*

'A lot of people are jumping onto the beer and food bandwagon now and it's great to see. There's a huge enthusiasm for it and that's perfect. People are going to discover the ideal combinations. The more people trying it then the more refined all our knowledge will be on the great combinations that are out there. I want beer to be part of the table and part of life's general experience.'

Phil Vickery,
*celebrity chef and landlord of the King of Prussia,
Farnham Royal, Buckinghamshire*

'I am very passionate about beer and food. I am a British chef and cook British food. Here we try and offer beers to go with the food. We have steak and kidney pie in Shepherd Neame's Spitfire and a spiced lamb pudding which is braised in the brewery's Early Bird. I have also enjoyed chocolate and fruit beers. When we opened our pub, we served Shepherd Neame's cherry fruit beer in champagne flute glasses and people loved it. I hate these archaic laws about half pints, a third of a pint, a gill – serve beer in shot glasses. Serving beer is a theatre. Anything I can do to match beer with food I am going to do.'

Michael Moore,
celebrity chef and owner of Michael Moore of Blandford Street, London

'I've been passionate about anything to do with food all my life, and am disappointed that beer doesn't get more room on the dining table in the UK. After all we are a beer country. Look at Belgium and Germany; they do it. I have travelled and cooked around the world for nearly 20 years and I lived and worked in beer countries such as Belgium and Germany and they thought beer and food was the right thing to do. There is a place for beers in restaurants providing the presentation is right. The secret is to serve it in small quantities, in schnapps style glasses. The UK has a great opportunity to be the number one in food and beer, because there are so many beers out there. Let us be proud about our beer.'

TABLE FOR TWO

Still not convinced about the pairing of beer and food? Here are two fine examples of imaginative menu-planning. Good beer and food matching is all about harmony of flavours, and these menus sailed through the test.

Caledonian Brewery Dinner for the British Guild of Beer Writers

Dish: beetroot-cured Scottish salmon with a petit herb salad, garnished with capers and lime.
Beer: Golden Promise (the world's first organic real ale), 5%
Tasting notes: rich and hoppy tangerine nose with a clean, dry and crisp taste; a tangy citric finish which invigorated the taste buds.
Why it worked: A very quenching beer whose freshness enabled it to meet and greet the oiliness of the salmon. The tangy finish merged with the herby flavours of the salad.

Dish: haggis with aged whisky drizzle.
Beer: Deuchars IPA (the brewery's championship beer), 3.8%
Tasting notes: aromatic and flowery on the nose with a great balance between a soft maltiness and emerging citrus hoppy notes on the palate with a dry and floral finish.
Why it worked: Beer, haggis and whisky all have barley as their base so there was a natural match while the citric hoppiness provided a counterpoint to the pepperiness of the haggis.

Dish: fillet of Scotch beef with Spanish onion jam, asparagus bundles and truffle-scented potato terrine.
Beer: 80/-, 4.1%
Tasting notes: malty and fruity aromas and a bready, malty, fruity palate. A dry, softly hoppy finish.
Why it worked: Stood up well to the broad palette of flavours on the plate and the slight sweetness within the beer fuses with the subtle sweetness of the well-hung beef.

Dish: Scottish cheeses.
Beer: Edinburgh Tattoo Strong Ale, 6.5%
Tasting notes: a complex strong ale with plenty of roast malt, vanilla, chocolate and even banana on the palate
Why it worked: the classic Scotch ale dovetailed perfectly with the cheese as the beer's many flavours matched and complemented the sharpness, saltiness and creaminess of the selection.

St Austell Tribute to Food and Beer at Pescadora, Padstow, Cornwall

Dish: oysters.
Beer: Warsteiner Pilsner, 5%
Tasting notes: pale yellow lager from Germany which has a dry palate leading to a refreshing hoppy finish.
Why it worked: stouts are traditionally served with oysters but this quenching and fresh tasting beer was a satisfying alternative with the dryness of the beer dovetailing with the saltiness of the bivalve.

Dish: fillet of Cornish sea bass served over steamed locally grown Pak Choi, spring onions and coconut rice cake furnished with a Thai red curry sauce.
Beer: St Austell's Clouded Yellow, 4.8%
Tasting notes: Bavarian-style wheat beer with bananas, creme brulée and bucket-loads of vanilla custard for the nose, followed by clove and bananas on the palate and a dry, fruity finish.

*Caledonian
Brewery
welcomes the
British Guild
of Beer Writers*

Why it worked: A case of sweet on sweet with the vanilla flavours of the beer going well with the coconut rice without overwhelming the delicacy of the sea bass.

Dish: baked fillet of Cornish cod topped with a basil and Yarg pesto crust served over refried beans spiced with chorizo sausage and finished with a roast tomato sauce.
Beer: Bridgeport IPA, 5.5%
Tasting notes: hoppy US IPA with a juicy soft malt palate, great citric hop attack and a lasting bitterness in the finish.
Why it worked: the hoppy bitterness and citric notes of the beer cut through the cassoulet's unctuousness, while spicy hop notes were a sensational match with the basil pesto crust and asserted themselves well against the meaty cod.

Dish: selection of Cornish cheeses.
Beer: Innis & Gunn Oak-Aged Beer, 6.6%.
Tasting notes: after 77 days aged in an oak barrel, this new-style beer has a vanilla and toffee palate and a very smooth finish.
Why it worked: the smoothness of the beer worked well with the creaminess of the cheeses, while the vanilla and toffee notes blended in with their subtle sweetness.

Dish: apple crumble with custard and rhubarb ice cream.
Beer: Liefman's Frambozen, 6.5%
Tasting notes: a fresh and fruity raspberry brown beer from Belgium with a lively spritzy character and a fragrant fruity nose.
Why it worked: the tart and fruity acidity of the beer complemented the creamy and sweet dessert but its fresh fruitiness also helped to clear the palate.

Digestive: Smuggler's Barley Wine, 8.5% Instead of a brandy or a port, St Austell's rare barley wine was served. Mahogany in colour, it has a roast, rum-like smoky, warming and alcoholic nose, while the palate served up nuts, malt and warming spirit-like notes with a subtly bitter finish.

Beer cocktails

Beer cocktails? Surely these are something unholy and the work of the Devil? Good beer is meant to be enjoyed on its own, unadulterated by anything that might upset the balance of hops and malt. What about mild and bitter, light and bitter, the students' favourite snakebite, and shandy (*Radler* in Germany, *panache* in France)? Then there are the so-called 'brewery blends' where a brewery will mix and match certain bitters. In America, some enterprising souls have risked their reputations by mixing barley wines with IPAs, fruit beers or wheat beers. More recently, bartenders in the hip haunts in London and New York, more used to mixing up measures of spirits, have turned to beer for new taste sensations. Whether these inventions are gimmicks or valid the jury is still out, but here are a few beer cocktails described for your information only!

Black and Tan – stout and mild

Black Velvet – stout and champagne

Shandy – bitter and lemonade, though Hoegaarden and lemonade is a refreshing alternative

Mild and Bitter

Dog's Nose – bitter and gin

Ginger Beer

Bitter Top – bitter with a splash of lemonade

Cooper – old term for mix of stout and porter

Broadway – beer and cola, popular in Japan

Skip and Go Naked – beer, lemon juice and gin, with a dash of grenadine for colour; apparently popular with American students

Depth Charge – a shot of whisky in stout

Beer Bloody Mary – bitter and tomato juice, with a dash of Tabasco and Worcestershire sauce

Red Eye – a shot of tomato juice in either an ale or lager, while a drop of Tabasco makes it a Ruddy Mary

Liverpool Kiss – stout with Cassis

Bee Sting – stout with orange juice

THERE'S A BEER FOR EVERY OCCASION

CELEBRATE WITH BEER

The sparkle of carbonation on the tongue; the elegant nose of fragrant hop and soft malt; the brisk waltz of flavours in the mouth; the light fantastic of pale gold in the glass. Beer is the life and soul of the party and throughout the ages it has accompanied communities as they celebrate life, the passing of the seasons, holy days, festivals, saint's days, harvests and weddings.

Beers for Christmas

Come Christmas lunch it's always assumed that wine has pride of place on the table. Why not change the habits of a lifetime and grab a beer instead? Kick-start the day and put the taste buds in a party mood with a bière de Champagne, a style of beer pioneered in Belgium and represented by Malheur Bière Brut (11%) or Deus (11.5%). These beers are produced in a similar way to champagne with re-fermentation in the bottle and a long period of maturation. They are big and complex beers with a spritzy and sparkling nose, followed by a palate that is herbal, citrusy and lemony, and finishing off with a tingling citrusy feel. On the other hand stay in the UK with a cool glass of Harviestoun's Bitter & Twisted (3.8% cask, 4.2% bottle). As this refreshing golden ale settles catch the escaping aromas of tropical fruit – very Carmen Miranda.

For starters, smoked salmon is the traditional dish. It requires a beer with enough hop bitterness and citrusy tang to cut through the oily texture and smoky flavours, leaving the palate refreshed and ready for the next mouthful. Try Young's Special London Ale (6.3%) or Fuller's ESB (5.5%). Turkey can be a bland old bird, even when tarted up with a herby stuffing and all the trimmings. Go for Fuller's bottle-conditioned 1845 (6.3%), where the roast malt, spicy hop and undercurrent of citrus fruit dovetail well with the turkey. Go really festive with Alaskan Winter Ale (6%), which is brewed with spruce tips. For the fruity Christmas pudding, choose a spicy, malty beer such as the bottle-conditioned Hail Mary (6%) from RCH or Otter Head (5.8%), a big tasting, flavoursome strong ale with toffee, rich malt and resiny hop aromas on the nose. Finally, say cheese. Put a hold on the port and go for Adnams' stupendous barley wine Tally Ho (7%). Otherwise Gale's bottle-conditioned Prize Old Ale (9%), Anchor's Old Foghorn (8.7%), Sierra Nevada's Bigfoot (10%), Lees Harvest Ale (11.5% and the older the better) or the well-matured Trappist beer Rochefort 10 (11.3%) are just the job.

New Year

Get the celebrations going with a fresh and fruity beer. Sean Franklin's Rooster's beers positively sing their hearts out with the scents of the hop garden. Try Scorcher (4.3%) or Hooligan (4.3%). Oakham's award-winning golden ale, JHB (3.8%) would be another choice. Or how about putting on the leather britches and going Bavarian with Schneider Weisse (5.4%). This classic wheat beer has plenty of bananas and cloves on the nose and a lively and fruity palate. And after Auld Lang Syne has been sung, how about a nip of Innis & Gunn's Oak-Aged Beer (6.6%), with its whisky warmth coming from a long maturation period in whisky barrels?

Halloween

While some go trick or treating, curl up with a good ghost story and a warming glass or two of Young's exceptional barley wine, Old Nick (7.2%) with its rich maltiness, warming glow on the palate and devilishly complex flavours full of apples, bananas and pear drops, all kept in order by a good hop character. Also try dark porter Exmoor Beast (6.6%) or Dogfish Head's Punkin' Ale (7%), which has real pumpkin and spices added to mash. Whatever you do, don't answer the door!

Bonfire night

Accompany your baked potatoes, roast sausages and toffee apples with Harvey's seasonal Bonfire Boy (5.8%), a smoky, spicy, warming rich beer whose subtle sweetness in the middle of the palate helps it to blend well with barbecued food. Also try Ventnor Brewery's Sandrock Smoked Ale (5.6%), Greene King's Strong Suffolk (6%) and Alaskan Smoked Porter (6.5%).

Thanksgiving

Joining friends or family for the turkey feast? Take along an American brown ale such as Brooklyn Brown Ale (5.5%) or Dogfish Head's Indian Brown Ale (7.2%). Their chewy, nutty and malty flavours pick a ride with the turkey's caramelised skin. In the absence of these beers, try a strong mild such as Teignworthy's Martha's Mild (5.3%) and Sarah Hughes Dark Ruby (6%), or go for O'Hanlons revivalist bitter Royal Oak (5%) – all three beers are available bottle-conditioned.

Anniversaries

For the first year together go frivolous and look for a light and sparkling beer such as Fenland Brewery's Sparkling Wit (4.5%), a fragrant and perfumy Belgian-style white beer brewed like an English ale. Also try Rebellion's White (4.5%), a Belgian-style wheat beer from Buckinghamshire which is packed with spice and zest. As the years progress, go for beers which can be aged, such as Fuller's Vintage Ale (8.5%), a rich and complex bottle-conditioned barley wine that gets more and more interesting with age – a perfect metaphor for the development of a relationship!

Birthdays

If you're giving beer as a gift splash out on an ale which will last the year. London microbrewery Pitfield look to the past for their splendid re-creation of classic beer styles and a gift pack of their bottle-conditioned 1850 London Porter (5%), 1837 India Pale Ale (7%) and 1792 Imperial Stout (9.3%) is a unique and unusual way of saying Happy Birthday to a beer lover. A brace of Thomas Hardy's Ales (11.7%), lovingly recreated by Devon brewers O'Hanlon's, delivered with the card, will also bring smiles to the face of a fan of John Barleycorn. In the party mood for drinking now? How about Timothy Taylor's Landlord (4.3%) or St Austell's Tribute (4.2%), both of which are fresh, tangy bitters with plenty of hoppy freshness and citrusy zing.

Weddings

Even though bride ales used to accompany the nuptials, it is more traditional nowadays for champagne or sparkling wine to be on hand to toast the bride and groom. Beer at a wedding is usually seen as fuel for the 'do' after the cake has been cut. However, be original and serve beer alongside the sparkling stuff and you'll be thanked by the beer-lovers in the crowd. Go for a light, spritzy golden ale with plenty of fruit on the nose. Serve Harviestoun's Bitter & Twisted (3.8%) or Fuller's Discovery (3.9%) in champagne flutes, slightly chilled; both are available in bottle. Or be really bold and get your hands on a case or two of Drie Fonteinen's Oude Gueuze (6%) with its funky fruity character.

Barbecue

Men think it macho to reach for a tin of lager when aprons are donned and tongs are waved as the barbecue is lit. Wrong. The smart set choose beer. Barbecued meat, fish and vegetables all have roast, smoky, sweet and spicy flavours (depending on the marinade) which demand robust beers to stand up to and then duel with. Step forward Greene King Abbot (5%) with its caramel and malt flavours eager to latch onto the chewy caramelisation of barbecued meats.

Also try St Peter's Suffolk Gold (4.9%), a full-bodied bitter with lasting hop aroma. There's plenty of fruit, toffee and caramel flavours in the middle which blend in well with the smoky sweetness of roast vegetables, while a long, spicy, dry and bitter finish helps to cleanse the palate for the next mouthful. Stone's Smoked Porter (5.9%) from the US is also a compelling companion. If it's fish you're grilling, then choose O'Hanlon's Double Champion Wheat Beer (4%), a seductively dry and zesty wheat beer which dovetails neatly with the sweetness of grilled haddock or sea bass.

Picnic

It's hot and there's time to be spent hanging out with friends by a river where the cool water can keep the beer chilled. The sun is shining and there are smoked chicken sandwiches, boiled eggs, cold meats and strawberries to be enjoyed. This is not the time for a strong porter or a ravishingly red ruby ale from Scotland. Remain north of the border though, with Arran Blonde (4.8%), a pale and aromatic beer from the Isle of Arran, whose soft malt character and flowery, gentle citrusy notes will blend in ideally with the smoked chicken. Alternatively, swoop on Oakham Ales' JHB (3.8%), an award-winning golden beer whose light, bubblegum fruitiness will cut through the spice and fat of the cold meats. Ready for the strawberries? Take a bottle of Meantime's Coffee Beer (4%) from the stream and enjoy its hints of vanilla and chocolate. Don't take your glassware to the picnic or drink from the bottle (you won't get the aroma), instead look for strong plastic glasses and you'll still get the joy of real beer in the open air.

Summertime

Heaven on earth is a beer garden on a hot summer's day with friends or family, savouring the prospect of one of the many summer ales now produced by British breweries. Golden ales are perfect for this time of the year, reflecting the sunlight (hopefully) and shimmering with flavour and aroma. Try Wye Valley's Dorothy Goodbody's Golden Ale (4.2%) from Herefordshire, which is as fruity as the fictional Dorothy, or the first ever golden ale Exmoor Gold (4.5%) from Somerset with its refreshing palate of soft malt and citrus followed by a subtle bitterness. For something stronger, pick up the splendidly thirst-

quenching, clean-tasting Summer Lightning (5%) from Hop Back, the all-time classic summer beer which you can drink all-year round to lighten up the darkest of days. Also try Rogue Younger's Special Bitter (4.8%), which sings with zingy tropical fruit aromas as well as the crisp tingle of biscuity malt.

Dinner Party

Call ahead and find out what's on the menu and plan accordingly. Big meaty dishes demand best bitters with plenty of fruit, malt and hoppiness. They also go well with meaty fishes such as tuna. How about Bateman's XXXB (4.8%) or a spicy and assertive Saison Dupont (6.5%) from Wallonia. On the other hand Thai or spicy dishes need a light and fragrant golden ale where the hoppiness is almost spicy or peppery. Try Hop Back's lemongrass beer Taiphoon (4.2%). Ice cream demands a fruit beer, try Meantime's bottle-conditioned Raspberry Wheat Beer (5%) or a Liefman's Kriek (6.5%), whose tissue bound bottle is certain to cause comment at the dinner table; also try dark strong stouts such as Harvey's Imperial Russian Stout (9%), where the chocolate and coffee flavours blend in superbly with ice cream and other creamy desserts. Also take along several bottles of your favourite barley wine such as bottle-conditioned Old Freddy Walker (7.3%), Gale's Prize Old Ale (9%), or Lees Harvest Ale (11.5%). Go for the wow factor with Anchor Brewery's star of a barley wine Old Foghorn (8.7%), to serve with the cheese.

Sunday lunch

The afternoon lies stretched ahead so there's no reason to rush. Welcome guests with a slightly chilled golden ale served in elegant glasses. Hobsons' Town Crier (4.5%) is available bottle-conditioned and is gorgeously fruity and easy to drink. Roast lamb deserves a beer with a slight sweetness in the background. Broughton's Old Jock (6.7%) is a powerful Scottish-style beer with plenty of rich fruit and maltiness to gambol along with the lamb, while on the lighter side of things the fresh maltiness and citrus tang of St Austell's Tribute (4.2%) will provide an interesting counterpoint. With roast beef, how about a strong pale ale such as Kelham Island's Pale Rider (5.2%), where zingy, fresh and fruity flavours will clear the palate after each rich mouthful; also try Adnams Broadside (4.5%) on draught if you can get hold of it from the pub. Vegetables are easy. Braise root vegetables in a dark stout such as RCH's Old Slug Porter (4.5%) and watch the sweetness of parsnips, turnips and carrots emerge blinking into the sunlight. Once more dessert and beer are a glorious match, with St Peter's Cream Stout (6.5%), Teignworthy's bottle-conditioned Empress Russian Porter (10.5%), Melbourne Brewery's unique Lincolnshire fruit beers (3.4%) and Samuel Smith's Oatmeal Stout (5%) all providing creamy and fruity reflections to most Sunday lunch desserts.

Let's order something in

Get a pizza in and ready yourself for Moorhouse's Black Cat Mild (3.4%) to work its magic. It sounds an odd combination but this dark and chewy mild with plenty of roast malt and chocolate flavours somehow latches onto the bready pizza base and the sweetness works well with spicy toppings. If you don't believe me, try it and see. Other notable milds worth sampling include Bateman's Dark Mild (3%) and Elgood's Black Dog Mild (3.6%). With fish and chips you need a beer with enough hop bitterness and flavour to cut through the oil and flour of the batter mixture, but not too much to drown the delicate flavour of the fish. The hoppiness also needs to be clean and fruity to stand up to the capers and malt vinegar in tartar sauce, plus a crisp sparkling mouth-feel for the seasonings. St Peter's Brewery in Suffolk use their Wheat Beer (4.7%) to make batter for their restaurant's fish and chips and it also works as an accompaniment. Also try O'Hanlon's Double Champion Wheat Beer (4%) and Kelham Island's Pale Rider (5.2%). With Indian food go for real IPAs with their spicy hop character. Marston's Old Empire (5.7%) or American IPAs from Goose Island (5.9%) or Sierra Nevada (5.6%) are sensational with Chicken Tikka. With Chinese food, try wheat beers such as Oakham's White Dwarf (4.3%) and honey beers such as Young's Waggle Dance (5%) and Conwy Brewery's Honey Fayre (4.5%) – the subtle honey notes of these beers chime superbly with sweet and sour pork. Badgers Blandford Fly (5.2%) has a hint of ginger to its flavour and this will hook onto the ginger and spices in your crispy duck. It's also a refreshing summer beer on its own.

A night in

Here you want easy drinking. If you're watching a film you don't want anything too strong or you may forget the ending. Something moreish and refreshing? How about Deuchars IPA (3.8%), with its balance of luscious soft malt and a quenching citrusy hoppiness, or maybe the fresh and firm flavours of Sam Adams' Boston Lager (5%).

At home with friends

These are beers to share, old favourites that you want to talk about while remembering great nights in the pub. Bitters from the likes of Bateman, Adnams and Hook Norton fit the bill, or you may want beers to amaze. How about speciality beers with honey, herbs, spices or fruit added? Try Skinner's Heligan Honey (4%) or, remaining on the Cornish peninsula, perhaps Blue Anchor's Spingo Bragget (6%), a hopless, honey ale which looks back to the Middle Ages for its inspiration. This Celtic duo will be stunning with relatively light dishes such as chicken satay or tempura prawns. For a bit of fruit, St Peter's produce five fruit beers (4.7%) including ones flavoured with elderberry, grapefruit and lemon and ginger. They also make a beer flavoured with nettles instead of hops. If you really want to get your friends talking serve them Williams' Fraoch (4.1%) from Scotland, a beer which is brewed with heather and based on a traditional Pictish recipe.

BEER
CURIOSITIES

The world of beer has a culture of its own,
from the etiquette of being served,
the choice of glass for a particular beer,
and the festivals that attract followers
all around the world.
BEER CURIOSITIES reveals how a
glass of beer can be the starting point for
a lifetime of exploration.

BEER ETIQUETTE

BAR BEHAVIOUR

When Britons need a drink they have to stand at the bar and catch the server's eye, sometimes waving money as if the prospect of exchanging cash for ale will cause quicker service. Vertical drinking is a term that refers to standing at the bar, glass in hand, chatting, mulling, reading the paper. Others prefer to retire to tables and chairs. Those with a busy-bodyish yen for telling drinkers what to do prefer the latter option with the belief that it moderates drinking.

In Europe, grab a table and wait for the beer waiter to amble over. In Northern France and Belgium, copies of the beer menu are handed out. Outdoors drinking is also more common across the English Channel. Tables spill out onto the pavement, while Bavarian beer gardens run riot with traditionally dressed waitresses and waiters serving brimming steins of Weisse and steaming plates of Wurst. In Prague's pubs, eagle-eyed waiters bring another beer as soon as a glass is emptied. It is not the done thing to pour an unfinished beer into another glass, by the way. Cologne is the home of Kölsch, which is served in the city's many bars by smartly dressed waiters who are nicknamed 'Kobes' and spend their time roaming the bar space with glasses of Kölsch on distinctive serving trays, ready to serve those who have run dry.

In America ordering a beer is very like the British experience, especially in East Coast bars, though West Coast etiquette involves more service. Brewpubs are a more formal experience with samples of the brewer's work sold in small glasses. Like all things that involve social interaction, the drinking of beer has its own rules and standards. What's yours?

Above: The serving of a pint should have a sense of theatre.

Left: The drinking of beer has its own rules and standards.

THE THEATRE OF THE SERVE

Whether beer is served by handpump, tap, jug or straight from a cask, there is always a great sense of anticipation as the glass starts to fill. Drinkers will be mesmerised watching the rising foam swirl around on top of the amber-coloured liquid. This is the defining moment for good real live beer – the serving of a pint should have a sense of theatre. A clean and attractive glass, a clear, sparkling pint with a collar of foam (its size and texture dependant on local bias), its arrival on the bar-top, the exchange of money (after all, this is a premium product worth paying for), that encounter with the first beer of the day. If it's a bitter then lick your lips as you wait for the biscuity maltiness, the hoppy fruitiness and the long bitter finish. Golden beer, stout, porter, barley wine, lager, lambic or IPA, it's always worth waiting for your favourite beer.

GUINNESS ART

The drama or display of serving beer was perfected by conscientious bar staff who used to etch an Irish harp into the foamy top of a pint of Guinness. Every pint of Guinness had to come with the signature of the person serving the beer. It might have been a promotional device on the part of the company (it is reputed that £8 million was spent training staff in the art of drawing the perfect pint), but it still looked good and made the drinker feel special.

The language of beer

Bottoms up, **cheers**, **chin chin**, **hwyl** (Welsh), **prost** (German), **slainté** (Irish) – colloquial toasts

Closing time – what the British landlord calls when he wants everyone to go home

Early doors – being at the pub at opening time

Guvnor – landlord of the British pub

Lock-in – when a pub continues to serve beer after the legal closing time

Mother in law (archaic) – old ale and bitter

My (your) shout – intention to buy the next round

Narfer narf (archaic) – slang from the East End of London which meant a half-pint of mild mixed in with the same amount of bitter

Round – a drinks order for more than one person

What's yours? – the opening words in the great British ritual of buying a round

A GLASS FOR EVERY BEER

GLASS DISTINCTIONS

The scene is a rundown cottage in the middle of the Lake District. The time is the fag end of the 1960s and a portly gentleman dispenses sherry to a couple of young out of work actors. 'I trust the shape will not offend your palate,' he says as three differing shapes of glasses are proffered. The scene is from the film *Withnail And I*, but the message is loud and clear. Wine and its family come in the right glasses. Imagine the same scene if Uncle Monty had been offering out libations of Bass or the local beer Jennings. The ales would probably have been served in tin cans and no apology offered.

The message behind this scene encapsulates the way beer has been served in times gone by, except by a few enlightened souls. Brandy demands the voluminous balloon to retire to the library with. Wine requires a variety of glasses whether burgundy, claret or a tall flute for an oaky Chardonnay. But what about beer? If you ask for a pint of beer, chances are you will receive it in what is called a nonic glass, which is straight-sided apart from a bulge like a spare tyre on a tummy two-thirds of the way up (the jut keeps the glass's rim from banging up against other rims when stored on a shelf). It can get even worse in restaurants where beer might be served in a tumbler better used for orange juice. Try asking the sommelier for a glass of house wine in a mug and watch his face, but he's quite happy to do the same with the beer.

Beer used to be offered in dimpled clear glass jugs, called handles, which may still be offered in some pubs, especially in rural areas. Their fans claim that the handle stops the beer from warming up. There remain a small number of pubs where an old regular has his

or her tankard hanging by the bar ready to receive their beer every night. Until the middle of the 19th century all beers would have been sold in such opaque containers, but when the tax on glass was lifted in 1845 drinkers could appreciate the golden sunlit hues of the then fashionable IPAs through clear glass.

There is a psychology behind the choice of glass. Half-pint nonic glasses are ugly and weedy looking, but the same volume in a taller, more elegant glass changes the perspective. The head retention of the beer is also affected by the shape of the glass. Glasses that taper inwards are preferred for foamy beers. This also helps to bring the aromas of the beer to the attention of your nose. Hoppy beers are especially welcome in such glasses.

Go to a Belgian bar and there will be a different glass for every type of beer you order. It has been known for drinkers to be refused their choice because no suitable glass is available. Trappist beers appear in goblet lookalikes while Duvel is served in a balloon-shaped receptacle resting on a flat-bottomed stem; this allows the drinker to appreciate the beer and the soft foamy head at the same time, while also savouring its fine aroma. Scottish ales have glasses in the shape of the thistle, Pilsners are served in tall, thin, wasp-waisted flutes, Abbey ales come in bowl-like glasses with a long stem and flat foot, while Kwak appears in a vessel that looks like a test-tube fitted into a wooden bracket, harking back to a time when

this was the easy way to hand coachmen their beer when they stopped for liquid refreshment. Much merriment is also gained for British drinkers from the fact that the De Koninck glass is called a Bolleke. In Germany wheat beers, Pilseners and Berliner Weisse all have their own elegant, long-legged supermodels of a glass, while American microbreweries are also getting in on the act. In Australia, ice-cold lager comes in schooners of different sizes according to the city in which the beer is served.

British bars and pubs are also seeing a renaissance of branded glasses. Fuller's launched a beautiful tulip-shaped glass with a long stem for ESB. Wadworth have small schooner style glasses for 6X. Innis & Gunn have also gone the glorious glassware route for their wood-aged beer, while breweries as diverse in size as Bath Ales, RCH and Badger offer up their beers in branded glasses. Devon brewers Otter offer appealing glasses with an image of an otter which owes more to Picasso than to Tarka.

The best glassware for the best long drink in the world should be the call. It's all about showing beer in the best possible light and getting the aroma, the condition, the look and the sound right. British beer quality assessors Cask Marque are trying to ensure that we have clean beer glasses (too much soapy detergent hampers head retention), so it's up to brewers, publicans and drinkers to make sure that we always have the right glass for the beer.

The phrase 'wet your whistle' comes from a time when beer mugs had whistles attached to their rims, which could be blown whenever a refill was needed – allegedly.

Glass act: there's a glass for every beer.

BEER FESTIVALS

AROUND THE WORLD IN A GLASS

In the early autumn of 1810 the residents of Munich celebrated the marriage of their Crown Prince and his new royal bride. Much beer was drunk and clearly someone thought they should do it more often as the Oktoberfest was born, though in the days before year-round brewing, September had always been the time when spring-brewed strong beers were finished off and new brews tapped with great enthusiasm. Whatever its origins, the Oktoberfest is the biggest event of its kind in the world.

The revival of real ale in 1970s Britain saw the emergence of national and regional beer festivals, as the success of CAMRA encouraged drinkers to try ales from far and near. These festivals were very different from the special exhibitions that brewers usually put on to promote their beers to the brewing industry and licensed trade – these were for the public.

Such beer festivals may be organised by CAMRA branches, local breweries, and organisations such as the Society of Independent Brewers (SIBA), a single pub with an enterprising landlord, or even a group of beer-loving individuals trying to raise money for charity. The number of beers sold can range from a dozen to hundreds. August sees the Great British Beer Festival at Olympia in London upon which tens of thousands of beer lovers converge in search of their favourite tipple.

In the US the Denver-based Great American Beer Festival, held in September or October, is a magnet for drinkers and brewers from around the world, while smaller festivals take place throughout the year around the States. The Extreme Beer Festival in Boston in January is a recent addition to this canon.

Despite its love of beer, Belgium has only recently joined the beer festival circuit, but you could argue that some beer cafés have their own festivals all year round. For instance, visit the Excelsior bar in the centre of Mons and over 50 beers are available to choose from. Whether in a municipal town hall, entertainment centre, historic building, tent city, beer garden, historic brewery or on the beach, wherever there's a beer festival there's good beer.

Above: The Oktoberfest is the largest beer festival in the world.

Right: Thousands of beer-lovers converge on the Great British Beer Festival in August.

Calendar of beer festivals

JANUARY
Great Alaskan Beer and Barley Wine Festival, Anchorage, Alaska, USA
CAMRA Winter Ales Festival, Manchester, England
Extreme Beer Festival, Boston, Massachusetts, USA

FEBRUARY
Battersea Beer Festival, London, England

MARCH
FAB Fest, Miami, Florida, USA
Zythos Bierfestival, Sint Niklaas, Belgium
London Drinker Beer and Cider Festival, London, England

APRIL
Maltings Beer Festival, Tuckers Maltings, Newton Abbot, England
New England Real Ale Exhibition, Somerville, Massachusetts, USA

MAY
Osaka Beer Festival, Osaka, Japan
Tokyo Beer Festival, Tokyo, Japan

JUNE
American Beer Festival, Boston, Massachusetts, USA

AUGUST
Great British Beer Festival, London, England
Berlin Beer Festival, Berlin, Germany
Peterborough Beer Festival, Peterborough, England

SEPTEMBER
Belgian Beer Weekend, Brussels, Belgium
Munich Oktoberfest, Munich, Germany

OCTOBER
Great American Beer Festival, Denver, Colorado, USA
PINT Bokbierfestival, Amsterdam, Netherlands

NOVEMBER
Winter Ales Festival, London, England

DECEMBER
Kerstbierfestival (Christmas Beer Festival), Essen, Belgium

Whether it's Munich, Antwerp or Tokyo, there's a beer festival for everyone.

ADVERTISING BEER

GOING AGAINST THE GRAIN – SELLING BEER

Any kind of enterprise has to advertise – and the beer business is no exception. British inns used to put out a long pole to tell passers-by when their ales were ready to be drunk. However, it wasn't until the 19th century that breweries started producing colourful posters and show-cards to entice drinkers to try their brown ales, pale ales, dinner ales, IPAs and oatmeal stouts.

During the 1930s British film stars were employed by Whitbread to suggest that their beers could be enjoyed at the restaurant table while dining in style. Meanwhile, drinkers throughout the world were also reminded that it was 'Guinness time': one surreal commercial shows six oysters crying their eyes out as the clock reaches 'Guinness time' and their end draws near. The advent of television saw advertisers go into overdrive. American viewers were told it was time for a Miller by a rugged, outdoors type, while the British learnt that a Double Diamond worked wonders and were encouraged to follow a dodgy looking bear in a trilby (the beer was an even dodgier lager called Hofmeister). With the onset of the designer age and governmental concerns about alcohol advertising, beer adverts became more surreal and sophisticated as exemplified by the stylish Guinness campaigns and the Euro-art film sheen of the Stella commercials, which promised a reassuringly expensive product.

As for the smaller family brewers in Britain, some have developed traditional themes, harking back nostalgically to the 'good old days'. The relaunch of Brakspears in Oxfordshire was accompanied by full colour posters of folk relaxing by the river. Incidentally, Refresh UK, who produce Brakspear, were also responsible for Wychwood's 'Lager boy'

advert, where a sinister ale-quaffing troll taunted lager-drinkers about their perceived lack of taste. Others prefer to go whacky: Wadworth's spent a fortune with suggestive posters about kinky 6X or 6X appeal, while old beery stereotypes died hard for St Austell in the form of a balding, tubby middle-aged man with his arms around a couple of much younger lovelies in swimwear to suggest that we needed a Tribute. In America, SAB-Miller and Anheuser-Busch looked to politics and launched so-called 'attack ads' on each other's products, while Russia has banned beer advertising altogether.

To end on a positive note, the best brewery advertisements of the last couple of years have come from Adnams, featuring simple coastal images centred around Adnams' unique provenance on the beautiful Suffolk Heritage Coast and designed to conjure up wonderful feelings of relaxation, refreshment, exuberance and quality of life. The beer's not bad either.

Like any other business, brewers have to advertise their wares.

If he can say as you can
Guinness is good for you
How grand to be a Toucan
Just think what Toucan do

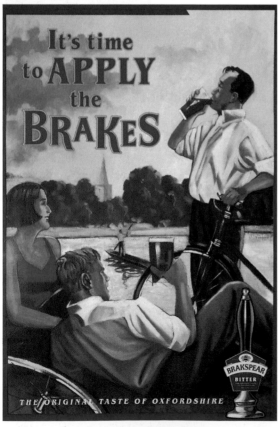

Beer advertising can be arty, cheeky, hearty or sentimental, as these examples from Adnams, Wadworth, Spaten and Brakspear show.

6X education

WHAT THE PUMP CLIP SAYS

You can't judge a book by its cover, apparently. However, when it comes to choosing a real ale at the bar a lot of drinkers go for the pump clip attached to the handpump. That is probably why breweries plump for garish colours, evocative images, silly names, and even flashing Santas to help sell their beers. Some pump clips are whacky, irreverent and almost cartoonish, while others go for the heritage look. A few licensees order up special pump clips decorated with cartoons of themselves. At the Blisland Inn in Cornwall, England, landlord Gary Marshall is caricatured with a pump clip for a beer called Fat God. Most clips contain details about the alcohol strength, so no excuses please if you've been on a session with something as Tysonesque as Robinson's Old Tom. Beneath the smirking old brewery cat there is the all important figure of 8.5%.

Even though breweries spend thousands of pounds advertising their products, it is the pump clip that is the front line of any advertising campaign. It is also very much in demand with small breweries on a tight budget. The bar is the point where the drinker interfaces (to use advertising jargon) with the product. According to John Ellis, ales brand manager at the Bedford family brewers Charles Wells, 'for real ale consumers, 71% of brand decisions are made at the bar – so the pump clip is a key player in the success of a brand.'

Pubs that sell a range of guest ales decorate their walls with used pump clips while serious collectors (who have yet to be given a proper name like labologists) pay equally serious sums for objects that used to be taken for granted. Like the beer mat, the pump clip is a reminder of a beer drunk and an evocation of the area and the pub where it was consumed. Pump clips appeared more commonly in British pubs during the 1950s when brewers realised that their beers represented brands and that something more was needed to push them at the point of sale. Before that, people were so used to asking for a pint of bitter or mild, that it wasn't necessary to give the product a name beyond X or XX or XXX. Pump clips have really came into their own during the microbrewer boom of the last 30 years – so let's face it; people do judge a book by its cover, no matter what the old proverb says.

The pump clip is the first thing a discerning drinker sees on approaching the bar. Few British pubs have this generous a selection of beers.

BEER MATS

Known as beer mats in the UK, coasters in the US, *Bierdeckel* in Germany and *sous-bocks* in France, drip mats were once made from cork, but nowadays are made from card. Breweries have always used them for promotional purposes, though advertising messages on beer mats in Sweden are banned. British beer-mat collectors call themselves 'tegestologists' and there is a Beer-mat Society with awards for the best beer mats.

COLLECTING BREWERIANA

Some people collect beer mats, others prefer pump clips or bar towels, and there are those who spend their spare time bartering for bottles. Bottle-tops, posters, brewery giveaways and trays get other folks' juices flowing. We're talking about breweriana, which is the word given to those collectible items associated with pubs, beer, brewing and drinking. Anything is fair game, from the above to ashtrays, adverts, beer labels and books. Especially desirable are pieces of breweriana linked with those companies now gone for good. Breweries even get in on the act themselves. George Bateman's fantastic bottle collection lines the walls at the brewery's visitor centre, while Gale's have managed to salvage a lot of their old pub signs and they are now displayed around the brewery. Most breweries with visitor centres offer an enticing collection of bottles, prints, labels and other artefacts. How to start a collection? There are specialist fairs while beer festivals run stalls with London's Olympia having the biggest of all. Also scour junk shops, especially in areas that used to have a brewery and, of course, there's always eBay.

The Collector

COLIN HEAPY has been collecting anything to do with beer and breweries since the mid 1970s, and he estimates that he has more than 9,000 different pump clips, 2,000 plus beer mats, 2,000 bottles and countless other memorabilia. He is a founder member of the Bottled Beer Collectors' Association.

'I started collecting in 1974 with the purchase of my first *CAMRA Good Beer Guide* and I have bought a copy of every one since. I also started visiting pubs and breweries then, recording all the beers drunk and photographing the breweries, so the next obvious step was something physical. I started with anything which had the brewery name: beer mat, pump clip or bottle. I had always been a collector. I believe that there are two types of people in the world: them that collect and them that don't. In 1977, the year of the Queen's Silver Jubilee, my bottle collection really took off with nearly 100 different breweries producing special bottles – I have them all. The Royal Wedding of 1981 saw over 150 different bottles produced, again I have them all.

The parts of my collection that I prize most are the ones with a story behind them; either how they were collected or who got them for me. For example, the bottle from Powys Brewery: the brewer had produced 48 bottles, and then died and the brewery closed. We contacted his wife and managed to purchase all 48 bottles for collectors for a donation to charity. Then there is the bottle from a Ugandan brewery. I was in Uganda and could drink the beer, but they would NOT sell me a bottle as these were worth much more than the beer. I eventually had to pay over $15 for the bottle while the beer was the equivalent of 50 US cents. The bottle did not even have a paper label as there was a paper shortage, however the crown cork did say Ugandan breweries.

As for the most valuable item it is difficult to say. Value is really down to the collector. Some items I would consider as my most precious are not valuable in monetary terms but in memories of how or where I got them. In monetary terms the Guinness items are rocketing in value. As for the rarest item in my collection – it's probably a pre-war metal enamel pump clip from Gartside's Brewery in Greater Manchester. It's the only one known to exist and was found after being thrown out into a skip behind an old labour club which was being refurbished. I love the thrill of the chase, trying to complete collections, which with all the new breweries is a never-ending task. There's also the fun of walking past your collection on show and remembering the fun, trauma and cost of obtaining each item.

I keep a lot of my collection in a purpose-built bar at home. I have had a bar in every house I have ever owned since 1975. I have also extended into the roof space and created a shelved room for bottles, pump clips and all my other breweriana. Other items are dotted all around the house where I have permission from my wife Jill.

The Holy Grail of breweriana really depends on what you collect. To get something nobody else has got is the ultimate buzz. It could be an old beer label, bottle, pump clip, jug or even an ashtray. For me though it would be anything from Walmersley Brewery in Bury, 200 yards from where I was born. It closed in 1927 and very little remains. Only a couple of beer labels are known about and they are very rare and expensive, should they ever be up for sale. I have only one old green bottle with the Walmersley name on it.'

BEER EDUCATION

GETTING THE KNOWLEDGE

Up until the launch of the British-based Beer Academy in 2003, the idea of beer education would have had sloppy barmen and women, lazy licensees and whiny wine snobs scratching their heads. Beer? Education? You could imagine their train of thought puffing away: it's wet, brown and goes down and you order another.

Breweries and organisations such as the British Institute of Innkeeping had been educating a select group of publicans for some years about the joys and complexities of beers and how to look after them. That was it though. Now it has all changed. For a start, the Beer Academy puts beer on the curriculum, while independent beer quality assessors Cask Marque ensure that real ale is dispensed correctly and award a plaque to pubs that pass their scheme. The brewing industry has woken up and realised that cask-ale drinkers care about their pint.

THE BEER ACADEMY

In the wine world the Wine and Spirit Education Trust was famous and respected for the way it dispensed knowledge to sommeliers, restaurateurs, journalists, wine-buyers and the general public. So it was to this august organisation that the beer world looked when the Beer Academy was first mooted in the winter of 2002. A year later, the Academy was up and running with the aim of helping beer-lovers and others learn about the nation's favourite drink. There is a choice of three courses: a two-and-a-half hour introductory one, a one-day Foundation Course and a three-day Advanced Course. The two longer courses have short exams. Those deterred by memories of school should

not be put off. These courses are intended to be fun and informative.

People are taught how to taste beer and match it with food, differentiate between the various ingredients and examine the broad range of beer styles available. Beer-lovers, journalists, pub and off-licence staff, brewery personnel, wholesalers and restaurateurs are among those who have taken part. Sponsorship comes from all sectors of the industry including regional brewers, pub chains and supermarkets, while support is given by the likes of CAMRA, the Society of Independent Brewers (SIBA), Cask Marque and the Wine and Spirit Education Trust.

CAMRA

Without the Campaign for Real Ale, there would be no real ale, and fizzy, flavourless beer would be our common lot. You might not even be reading this book. Opening time began in 1971, when four English drinkers on holiday in Ireland were bemoaning the state of ale back home. They decided to do something about it and formed the Campaign for the Revitalisation of Ale. It was a bit of a laugh at first but twanged a chord amongst drinkers fed up with their favourite pubs being gutted and turned into chintzy living rooms, while locally brewed beers were replaced by gassy products brought in from factories hundreds of miles away.

By 1973, 1,000 members had signed the pledge to save British beer, but the original title was seen as too much of a mouthful and so the Campaign for Real Ale was born. Since then it has fought pub and brewery closures, celebrated the small brewers' boom,

**CAMPAIGN
FOR
REAL ALE**

held hundreds of beer festivals across the country, lobbied governments about such issues as the beer orders, short measures, opening times and guest ales; promoted beer and food and generally saved British cask-conditioned ale from becoming a small minority taste such as pear perry or mead. These days the membership is over 80,000 and the organisation has done a lot to shed its beer bellies and woolly jumper image – at least 25% of the membership is female.

As a campaigning group, CAMRA is unparalleled in the brewing world, and it can be claimed that it has influenced small brewers across the world, especially in America. Its showpiece celebration of all that's good and great in beer, the Great British Beer Festival, is held every August in London, and it publishes a newspaper, *What's Brewing*, where you can keep abreast of what is going on in the brewing world. Fellow European beer consumer groups include the Association for Promotion and Information about Traditional Beer (PINT) based in Holland and Zythos in Belgium.

BRITISH GUILD OF BEER WRITERS

It's a hard job but someone has to keep an eye on the brewing industry and its shenanigans, record all the great beers that sustain the beer-loving world and celebrate the eccentricities and glories of the British pub. This is where the British Guild of Beer Writers comes in use and here you will find a wide range of members with one thing in common – a love of John Barleycorn and a passion to bring it to a wider audience. The Guild has been going since the 1980s and its members visit breweries, organise tastings and hold regular seminars on all aspects of beer, from the new wave IPAs to the time-travelling antics of the Durden Beer Circle. There is an annual dinner every December when the awards for the beer writers of the year are dished out.

BREWERS' ORGANISATIONS

The older, more established breweries, otherwise known as regional or family breweries, gather together in the Independent Family Brewers of Britain, while smaller and more recent brewers do business under the umbrella of the Society of

Independent Brewers (SIBA). In America, many of the craft brewers are represented by the Association of Brewers, while the American Homebrewers Association looks after the interests of its members, many of whom go on to become commercial brewers.

Durden Park Beer Circle

Lots of microbrewers started off simply making their own beer at home, inviting friends round for sampling sessions before going commercial. A small intrepid band of enthusiasts gathered together in 1971 to form the legendary Durden Park Beer Circle. They are the time-travellers of beer. Their mission is to explore the long lost beer recipes and styles of the past and, where possible, to bring them back to life. The aim was to improve the practice of home brewing, which meant that brewers gave talks, comparative tastings were held and lots of beers from around the world were sampled. Meanwhile brewing books and recipes were consulted and archives rifled through. The results have been a constant stream of resurrected old beer styles. Back in the 1970s, one of the members gave a glass to an elderly lady who usually had a Guinness before lunch. It was actually an 1859 porter and when the guinea pig took a sip she exclaimed 'This isn't Guinness, it's London porter'. 'We can never be sure for certain that we are emulating the beers of the 1850s,' says Geoff Cooper from the Circle, 'but we can't be far off as that elderly lady suggested.'

In 2002 the Circle hosted a seminar for the British Guild of Beer Writers at the Brewers Hall in London. By then they had 50 members and possessed 630 different beer recipes. After the information and passion generated by the members' talk, writers were treated to a stunning array of beers re-created from the 19th century. There were several porters, a Russian Imperial stout, brown ales, bitters and an IPA. The beers had an elegance and substantial sense of flavour and character. A Simmonds Reading Bitter from the 1850s was rich with maltiness, which was balanced with a spiky, lasting hoppy bitterness. These were all memorable beers, rhapsodised about by those present long after the taste had faded away. Such beers are part of our brewing heritage and, thanks to the Durden Park Circle, they are not dead yet.

BEER FOR LIFE

GOOD HEALTH!

Grab a glass of beer and drink yourself healthy. Recent findings imply that beer can indeed be seriously good for your health. Contrary to popular opinion, a 'beer belly' is not the result of too much ale: blame it on the curries or bags of chips on the way home from the pub. Your innocent pint contains 190 kilocalories while your average Indian meal weighs in at a belt-straining 1,000 kilocalories. Still feeling peckish? A cheeseburger and chips has 962 kilocalories while steak and kidney pie, chips and beans packs in 700 kilocalories. Scientists around the globe are discovering that the other old chestnut, beer is bad for you, is another myth. A pint a day might even keep the doctor away, though it must be stressed that the health benefits of beer are all about moderate consumption.

GETTING PHYSICAL

The love of good beer is the magnet that draws people to explore the Quantock Hills in Somerset. Ian Pearson and Lynne Abbott quit London in 2003 and headed west to run their unique real ale rambles. Spend a weekend with them in the sleepy old village of Nether Stowey and trek across the beautiful landscape of the Quantocks while enjoying pub lunches in such venerable inns as the Carew Arms at Crowcombe. Come evening visit another excellent country pub, before returning for dinner served alongside local beers. Meanwhile, mountain bikers with a love of ale should make their way to Llanwrtyd Wells, a small town in the hills of Powys, South Wales. The Real Ale Wobble is an annual event held

in November in conjunction with the Mid-Wales Beer Festival. Choose between 15, 25 or 40 miles each day, with all routes clearly marked. Register and enjoy free half pints of real ale at the checkpoints. All routes are off-road, using farm and forest tracks, paths, open land, wild and desolate mountain terrain. In the evening, wash off the mud and relax with another pint or two. Beats the gym and a personal trainer any day.

A glass of beer a day might keep the doctor away.

Doctor's orders

Consider the following impressive facts that medical research has uncovered next time you order a beer

- A potent, cancer fighting antioxidant called xanthohumol is found in hops. Studies show that it is able to stem the growth of tumour cells. Beer contains twice as many antioxidants as wine. These are thought to reduce the risk of heart attacks by curbing blood clotting.

- Researchers commissioned by a Japanese brewery have discovered that the development of fat inside the body could be inhibited by a bittering element in hops.

- Dutch doctors announced that moderate drinking can help to protect against artery disease.

- The cell walls of malted barley are a source of soluble fibre. This slows down food absorption and reduces cholesterol levels, which may help to lessen the risk of heart disease. It also helps to keep you regular!

- Vitamins B6 and B9 are both found in beer and can help to give beer-lovers protection against cardiovascular disease.

- Beer is high in potassium and low in sodium, just the right balance for a healthy blood pressure.

- A pint a day could help to strengthen bones, thanks to the presence of silicon in the barley that goes into your beer.

- Kidney disease and gallstones may be kept at bay as beer is low in calcium and rich in magnesium. A daily beer is thought to help reduce the risk of kidney stones by 40%.

- Hambleton Ales in Yorkshire have developed a gluten- and wheat-free beer aimed at gluten-intolerant drinkers.

- Beer contains zero fat and zero cholesterol.

- A glass of beer at the end of the day helps to relax both the mind and the body; hops are a potent sedative for nervous tension and anxiety. Hops can help to settle a nervous stomach and may even soothe Irritable Bowel Syndrome (IBS).

TASTING NOTES

If you've got this far then I suspect you fancy a beer. Why not go one step further and use these pages to jot down your impressions of some of the beers you've tasted. Turn to page 29 on 'The 10 Steps to Heaven'. Enjoy.

NAME	BEER STYLE	COUNTRY	STRENGTH	COLOUR

AROMA	TASTE	FINISH	OVERALL SCORE

GLOSSARY

ABV
A standard scale of alcoholic strength, otherwise known as alcohol by volume, which is a guide to the percentage of alcohol in a finished beer. Alcohol by weight is the measure used in the American brewing industry.

Adjuncts
Additions to the mash such as wheat flour, rice, corn, maize or sorghum, these are usually employed for reasons of cost or to make a beer lighter in body.

Ale
The name derives from the Anglo-Saxon *ealu*, which was originally a malted alcoholic drink with added herbs and spices to clarify, season or preserve it. Up until the introduction of hops in Britain, the words beer and ale were interchangeable. Afterwards, beer came to mean the hopped variant.

Alpha acid
The component in the hop that produces bitterness. The higher the alpha acid, the more bitter the hop.

Aroma hops
Hops used for their aromatic quality. They are low in alpha acids and put into the boil in the latter stages.

Attenuation
The degree to which fermentable sugars are changed into alcohol and carbon dioxide by yeast during fermentation. The more attenuation, the drier and stronger the beer.

Barley
A cereal crop that produces grain in the same way as a tree will produce berries, fruit or nuts. When the grain is part germinated and kilned it produces malted barley, which is used in the first step in brewing.

Barrel
Lay-person's term for a nine-gallon cask of beer, while those in the trade talk of a firkin. In the brewery a barrel is 36 gallons and a measure of the brew-length of a brewery. In the American brewing industry a barrel is 31.5 gallons. In Europe the capacity of a brewer is measured in hectolitres.

Beer
Derived from the Anglo-Saxon word *beor*, the term 'beer' was interchangeable with ale until the appearance of hops. Beer denotes a beverage produced by fermented grain, chiefly malt, which has been hopped.

Bittering hops
Hops high in alpha acids which give bitterness to the flavour of beer. They are added at the start of the boil. Also called copper hops and kettle hops.

Bottom-fermentation
Fermentation that takes place at a low temperature, with yeast sinking to the bottom of the vessel. Generally used for lagers and also known (perhaps more accurately) as cold-fermentation.

Burtonisation
This brewing process began in the 19th century (and continues today) whereby mineral salts similar to those found naturally in Burton-on-Trent's local water were added to the brewing liquor by other brewers eager to replicate Burton's beers.

Cooper
Beer was traditionally kept in wooden casks and the cooper was the man who made and repaired these casks. Today the number of coopers can almost be counted on one hand.

Copper
The brewing vessel in which the wort is boiled and hops and other flavourings are added. Also called the kettle.

Decoction mashing
Method of mashing used for lager brewing where some of the wort is taken out, heated up and added back to the mash.

Dry hopping
Practice of adding a handful of hops (or hop pellet) to beer in the cask.

Esters
These volatile flavour compounds are produced by the work of the yeast on fermenting beer. They often produce a fruity (banana/pear) complexity in both aroma and taste.

Finings
Liquid which is added after cask-conditioned beer is racked into cask to help to clear it. It attracts the yeast in the cask and the two of them sink clasped together to the bottom. Finings are traditionally made from the swim bladder of the sturgeon fish, though other members of the sturgeon family are pressed into action these days.

Firkin
A nine-gallon cask. The next size is double at 18 gallons, called a kilderkin, followed by the rarely used hogshead holding 36 gallons. The vanished puncheon and butt held 72 and 108 gallons respectively.

Grist
Crushed or milled barley malt ready to be mashed as the first part of the brewing process.

IBU
Otherwise known as International Units of Bitterness, a scale that measures the bitterness of beer.

Kilning
The process where the partially germinated malt is dried in massive maltings kilns. Next stop the mill and then the mash tun.

Kräusen
Process taking place during lager maturation (or lagering) where partially fermented wort is added to the brew with the aim of geeing up the secondary fermentation.

Lagering
Period of maturation for lager (in German, *lager* means 'to store'). The method is supposed to have originated in 15th-century Bavaria when beers were stored in cool caves, where the temperature encouraged a slower mode of fermentation.

Mash
Process where milled malt is steeped in hot liquor in a mash tun for the purpose of extracting fermentable sugars. This takes several hours and is aided by sparging (or spraying) the mash (as it is known) with hot water to get out all the fermentable sugars. The result is called the sweet wort.

Original gravity
Unit of measurement of the strength of a beer, based on the amount of dissolved fermentable malt sugars present in the wort after the mash has taken place. Water is defined as having an original gravity of 1000, so a beer with an original gravity of 1040 (the usual amount for ordinary bitter) is approximately 4% denser than the water.

Pasteurisation
Once beer is brewed it can be left to continue its secondary fermentation or it can be filtered and pasteurised before being bottled, canned or kegged. Named after Louis Pasteur, pasteurisation involves treating filtered beer with heat for the purpose of killing off any remaining yeast cells.

Pilsner
The world-beating golden lager gets its name from the Czech city of Pilsen (or Plzeň in the native tongue), where it was developed in 1842. It simply means 'from Pilsen'. German variations on the spelling give us Pilsener and Pils, the latter being in common usage for lager-style beers, many of which have little character.

Rack
The process when finished beer is put into the cask from the fermenting vessels or conditioning tanks.

Real ale
Real, living beer. Before the onset of kegged beers in the 1960s, all beer was real, undergoing a secondary fermentation in the cask. The term 'real ale', however, was coined in the 1970s by CAMRA as they launched a campaign against the fizzy, dead beers that were gradually supplanting traditional beers. Nowadays, the term means beer that matures in the cask and does not have extraneous carbon dioxide. Also called cask-conditioned.

Secondary fermentation
Primary fermentation occurs during the brewing process when yeast is pitched into the hopped wort. When real ale is racked into casks there is always enough residual yeast for a secondary fermentation to continue, developing the flavour and condition of the beer.

Sparging
After the mash is finished, the malt is sparged (or sprayed) with hot water to extract any remaining sugars.

Top-fermenting
The fermentation process used for British ales and certain German beers such as Weisse, Alt and Kölsch, with the yeast working at 15-20°C. Not all sugars are fermented, which results in a fruitier, sweeter beer than those that undergo bottom-fermentation. Also known as warm-fermenting.

Tun
Originally this was a brewing container of several hundred gallons, but the term is now used in conjunction with certain brewing vessels, such as the mash tun.

Union system
Unique method of fermentation involving the use of oak barrels which is now solely in use at Marston's Brewery, Burton-on-Trent.

Wort
The liquid that remains after mashing. It tastes malty and is full of malt sugars. Next stop the copper where it will be boiled with hops.

FURTHER READING

Ale Trail, The: Roger Protz, Eric Dobby Publishing, 1995

Book About Beer, A: A Drinker, Jonathan Cape, 1934

Beer: Michael Jackson, Dorling Kindersley, 1998

Beer Companion: Michael Jackson, Mitchell Beazley, 1997

Beer Cookbook, The: Susan Nowak, Faber & Faber, 1999

Beer Drinkers Companion, The: Frank Baillie, David & Charles, 1973

Beer In Britain: Various, Times Publishing Company, 1960

Beer Memorabilia: Martyn Cornell, Apple, 2000

Beer: The Story of the Pint: Martyn Cornell, Headline, 2003

Belgo Cookbook: Denis Blais & André Plisnier, Phoenix Illustrated, 1998

Book of Beer, The: Andrew Campbell, Dennis Dobson, 1956

Brewer's Art, The: B Meredith Brown, Whitbread & Co, 1948

Brewing up a Business: Sam Calagione, Wiley & Sons, 2005

Brewmaster's Table, The: Oliver Garrett, Harper Collins, 2003

Century of British Brewers Plus 1890–2004, A: Norman Barber, Brewery History Society, 2005

Country Ales and Brewers: Roger Protz, Steve Sharples, Weidenfeld & Nicolson, 1999

Drink: Andrew Barr, Bantam, 1995

Encyclopaedia of Beer: editor Christine Rhodes, Henry Holt, 1995

English Pub: A History, The: Peter Haydon, Hale, 1994

Good Beer Guide: CAMRA Books

Good Beer Guide Belgium: Tim Webb, CAMRA Books, 2005

Great Beers of Belgium, The: Michael Jackson, Prion, 1998

India Pale Ale: Roger Protz, Clive La Pensée, CAMRA Books, 2001

Inn-Signia: Brian Hill, Whitbread & Co, 1948

Lagerlagerlager: Ted Bruning, unpublished

Licensed to Sell: the History and Heritage of the Public House: Geoff Brandwood, English Heritage, 2004

Old British Beers and How To Make Them: various, Durden Park Beer Circle, 2003

Prince of Ales: Brian Glover, Alan Sutton Publishing, 1993

Pub: Angus McGill (ed), Longmans, 1969

Short History of Ale, A: Jimmy Young, David & Charles, 1979

Slow Food, Collected Writings on Taste, Tradition and the Honest Pleasures of Food: Various, Grub Street, 2003

Taste of Beer, The: Roger Protz, Weidenfeld & Nicolson, 1998

Time, Gentlemen, Please! Early Brewery Posters in the Public Record Office: Michael Jones, Pro Publications, 1997

Traditional English Pub, The: Ben Davis, Architectural Press, 1981

Travels With Barley: Ken Wells, Wall Street Journal Books, 2004

Ultimate Encyclopaedia of Beer, The: Roger Protz, Ted Smart, 1995

Victorian Pubs: Mark Girouard, Yale, 1984

You Brew Good Ale: Ian R Peaty, Sutton Publishing, 1997

West Country Ales: Adrian Tierney-Jones, Halsgrove, 2002

Word For Word: An Encyclopaedia of Beer: Whitbread & Co, 1953

World Encyclopaedia of Beer: Brian Glover, Select Editions, 1997

You Brew Good Ale: Ian R Peaty, Sutton Publishing, 1997

WEBSITES

Most breweries across the world have their own websites which are worth exploring. Here is a selection of other informative sites.

www.alestreetnews.com
www.allaboutbeer.com
www.beeracademy.org
www.beeradvocate.com
www.beerhunter
www.beerinnprint.co.uk
www.beermad.org.uk
www.beerme.com
www.beer-pages.com
www.beerwriters.co.uk
www.bottledbeer.co.uk
www.breweryhistory.com
www.camra.org.uk
www.eastanglianbrewers.com
www.maxbeer.org
www.quaffale.org.uk
www.realbeer.com
www.worldofbeer.com

INDEX

AUTHOR'S ACKNOWLEDGEMENTS

I would like to thank the following for putting up with my queries, requests for pictures and any other strange demands. Anyone I have missed out, I will buy you a pint... Ted Bruning, Mark Dorber, Jeff Evans, Tim Hampson, Steve Hobden, Teddy Maufe, Sue Nowak, Thomas Perera, Rupert Ponsonby, Mike Powell-Evans, Roger Ryman, John White ... and not forgetting Jane and James who have to put up with a lot of beer stuff.

PICTURE ACKNOWLEDGEMENTS

8 Mark Turner; 12 CAMRA Archive; 14 AKG-images/Nimatallah; 15 above AKG-images; 15 below Mary Evans Picture Library; 16 left Zefa/K Hackenberg; 16 centre Adrian Tierney-Jones; 16 right Mark Turner; 17 above Adrian Tierney Jones; below left John Boxall; 18 Mark Turner; 19 above Mary Evans Picture Library; 19 below left Zefa/G. Rossenbach; 19 below right Adrian Tierney-Jones; 20 Adrian Tierney-Jones; 21 Mark Turner; 22 Tetleys Brewery; 23 Zefa /E. Koch; 24 Caledonian Brewing Company; 25 Photononstop; 26 Mark Turner; 28 Samuel Smith Old Brewery; 30 Cephas/Stockfood; 31 left CAMRA Archive; 31 right Rogue Brewery; 32 left George Gale & Co.; 32 centre Fuller, Smith & Turner; 32 right Marston, Thompson & Evershed; 33 above CAMRA Archive; 33 below George Bateman & Son; 34 above Photolibrary.com/Peter Adams/Jon Arnold Images; 34 below St Peter's Brewery; 35 CAMRA Archive; 36 left CAMRA/ Vanessa Courtier; 36 right CAMRA Archive; 37 above CAMRA Archive; 37 below Belhaven Brewing Co.; 39 above Cephas/Nigel Blythe; 39 below Rex Features/Paul Cooper; 40 left Obergarige Hausbrauerei Zum Uerige; 40 right Paulaner-Salvator-Thomasbräu; 41 left CAMRA/Vanessa Courtier; 41 centre Cephas/Joris Luyten; 41 right Budvaruk.com; 42 left Sierra Nevada Brewing Company; 42 right Brooklyn Brewery; 43 Alaskan Brewing Company; 44 above & below right Adrian Tierney-Jones; 44 left CAMRA/Vanessa Courtier; 45 left Photononstop /Soleil Noir; 45 right Brasserie Duyck; 46 CAMRA/Vanessa Courtier; 47 Zefa/Sucré Salé; 49 Greene King; 50–51 Innis & Gunn Brewing Co.; 52 Adrian Tierney-Jones; 55 CAMRA Archive; 57 Hobsons Brewery & Co.; 58 CAMRA Archive; 59 Brakspear Brewing Co.; 60 Adrian Tierney-Jones; 61 Moorhouses Brewery; 61 below Adrian Tierney-Jones; 62 Adrian Tierney-Jones; 63 Meantime Brewing Co.; 65 George Bateman & Son; 68–69 St Austell Brewery; 70 Adrian Tierney-Jones; 71 CAMRA Archive; 72 Thornbridge Brewery; 73 St Peter's Brewery; 74 above left CAMRA Archive; 74 above right, below & 75 Plzensky Prazdroj; 76 left AKG-images; 76 right Cephas/Nigel Blythe; 77 left Zefa/Stock4b/Andreas Korner; 77 right Adrian Tierney-Jones; 78–79 Elgoods Brewery; 80 The Dalesman; 81 O'Hanlons Brewery Co.; 82 Collection Hémispheres; 84–85 John Heseltine; 85 above left Collections; 85 above right Corbis/ Gary Houlder; 86–87 Anthony Blake Picture Library/Mark Turner; 89 Photononstop/Benelux Press; 90 Oakham Ales; 91 The White Horse, Parsons Green; 93 Photononstop/Tristan Deschamps; 94 above Adrian Tierney-Jones; 94 below Rex Features/Ilpo Musto; 96 Retna/Walter McBride; 97 above Adrian Tierney-Jones; 97 below Karl Blackwell; 98–99 Corbis/Homer Sykes; 99 above left Corbis/Annie Griffiths Belt; 99 above right Photolibrary.com/J Curve; 100 CAMRA Archive; 101 Superstock/ age fotostock; 102 Coors Brewers; 103 above CAMRA Archive; 103 centre Sierra Nevada Brewing Co.; 103 below O'Hanlon's Brewery; 104–105 CAMRA Archive; 106 Cephas/Stockfood; 109 Corbis/Nik Wheeler; 110 Badger Brewery; 111 The White Horse, Parsons Green;114 CAMRA Archive 115 top Adrian Tierney-Jones; 115 centre Rex Features/Dave Penman; 115 bottom Michael Moore; 116 Caledonian Brewery; 119 Cephas/Stockfood; 120 Photononstop; 121 Zefa/Hein van den Heuvel; 123 Corbis/Zefa/ Auslöser; 124 Mary Evans Picture Library; 126 Photolibrary.com; 127 Topfoto; 128 Photononstop/Hubert Paul; 129 left Fuller, Smith & Turner; 129 centre De Koninck Brouwerij; 129 right Brouwerij Bosteels; 130 Alamy/allOver Photography; 131 CAMRA Archive/Hazel Dunlop; 132 above Zefa/H. Spichtingen; 132–133 O.B.E.R.; 133 above Great American Beer Festival; 133 centre Japan Craft Beer; 134 Adnams; 135 above left Cephas/ M. J. Kielty; 135 above right Advertising Archives; 135 centre right Karl Blackwell; 135 below left CAMRA Archive; 135 below right Cephas/M. J. Kielty; 136 above Adnams; 136 below left Brakspear Brewing Co.; 136 below right Mary Evans Picture Library; 137 above Photononstop/Mauritius; 137 below Wadworth & Co.; 138 far left Grolsche Bierbrouwerij; 138 left St Peters Brewery; 138 right CAMRA/Vanessa Courtier; 138 far right CAMRA/ Vanessa Courtier; 139 centre Hobsons Brewery & Co.; 139 left CAMRA Archive; 139 right Caledonian Brewing Company; 140 Mark Turner; 141 CAMRA Archive; 142 CAMRA/Hazel Dunlop; 143 Adrian Tierney-Jones; 146 Images of France/Jan Isachsen; 147 Photolibrary.com/Foodpix.

BOOKS FOR BEER-LOVERS

CAMRA Books, the publishing arm of the Campaign for Real Ale, is the leading publisher of books on beer and pubs. Key titles include:

Good Beer Guide 2006

Editor: ROGER PROTZ

The Good Beer Guide is the only guide you will need to find the right pint, in the right place, every time. It's the original and the best independent guide to around 4,500 pubs throughout the UK; the Sun newspaper rated the 2004 edition in the top 20 books of all time! Now in its 34th year, this annual publication is a comprehensive and informative guide to the best real ale pubs in the UK, researched and written exclusively by CAMRA members and fully updated every year.

£13.99   ISBN 1 85249 211 2

300 Beers to Try Before You Die

ROGER PROTZ

300 beers from around the world, handpicked by award-winning journalist, author and broadcaster Roger Protz to try before you die! A comprehensive portfolio of top beers from the smallest microbreweries in the United States to family-run British breweries and the world's largest brands. This book is indispensable for both beer novices and aficionados.

£12.99   ISBN 1 85249 213 9

CAMRA'S Good Cider Guide

The 5th edition of this title features more than 600 traditional cider producers and outlets in the UK and is an essential volume for anyone wishing to become a cider connoisseur. The popularity of real cider is permanently rising, as more and more people discover how deliciously mellow, aromatic and intoxicating the flavours of naturally-produced cider can be. CAMRA'S Good Cider Guide, revised and updated, offers a county-by-county directory of UK cider producers and outlets and provides unique, in-depth knowledge for the discerning cider consumer.

£10.99   ISBN 1 85249 195 7

The Book of Beer Knowledge

JEFF EVANS

A unique collection of entertaining trivia and essential wisdom, this is the perfect gift for beer lovers everywhere. More than 200 entries cover everything from the fictional 'celebrity landlords' of soap pubs to the harsh facts detailing the world's biggest brewers; from bizarre beer names to the serious subject of fermentation.

£9.99   ISBN 1 85249 198 1

Good Beer Guide Belgium

Editor: TIM WEBB

Now in its 5th edition and in full colour, this book has developed a cult following among committed beer lovers and beer tourists. It is the definitive, totally independent guide to understanding and finding the best of Belgian beer and an essential companion for any beer drinker visiting Belgium or seeking out Belgian beer in Britain. Includes details of the 120 breweries and over 800 beers in regular production, as well as 500 of the best hand-picked cafes in Belgium.

£12.99   ISBN 1 85249 210 4

Good Beer Guide Germany

STEVE THOMAS

The first ever comprehensive region-by-region guide to Germany's brewers, beer and outlets. Includes more than 1,200 breweries, 1,000 brewery taps and 7,200 beers. Complete with useful travel information on how to get there, informative essays on German beer and brewing plus beer festival listings. To be published in June 2006.

£14.99   ISBN 1 85249 219 8

Order these and other CAMRA books online at **www.camra.org.uk/books**, ask at your local bookstore, or contact: CAMRA, 230 Hatfield Road, St Albans, AL1 4LW. *Telephone* 01727 867201

IT TAKES ALL SORTS TO CAMPAIGN FOR REAL ALE

CAMRA, the Campaign for Real Ale, is an independent not-for-profit, volunteer-led consumer group. We actively campaign for full pints and more flexible licensing hours, as well as protecting the 'local' pub and lobbying government to champion pub-goers' rights.

CAMRA has 80,000 members from all ages and backgrounds, brought together by a common belief in the issues that CAMRA deals with and their love of good quality British beer. For just £18 a year, that's less than a pint a month, you can join CAMRA and enjoy the following benefits:

A monthly colour newspaper informing you about beer and pub news and detailing events and beer festivals around the country.

Free or reduced entry to over 140 national, regional and local beer festivals.

Money off many of our publications including the *Good Beer Guide* and the *Good Bottled Beer Guide*.

Access to a members-only section of our national website, **www.camra.org.uk** which gives up-to-the-minute news stories and includes a special offer section with regular features saving money on beer and trips away.

The opportunity to campaign to save pubs under threat of closure, for pubs to be open when people want to drink and a reduction in beer duty that will help Britain's brewing industry survive.

Log onto **www.camra.org.uk** for CAMRA membership information.

**CAMPAIGN
FOR
REAL ALE**

DO YOU FEEL PASSIONATELY ABOUT YOUR PINT? THEN WHY NOT JOIN CAMRA

Just fill in the application form (or a photocopy of it) and the Direct Debit form on the next page to receive three months' membership FREE!

If you wish to join but do not want to pay by Direct Debit, please fill in the application form below and send a cheque, payable to CAMRA, to:
CAMRA, 230 Hatfield Road, St Albans, Hertfordshire AL1 4LW.

Please tick appropriate box

☐ Single Membership (UK & EU) £18

☐ For under-26 Membership £10

☐ For 60 and over Membership £10

For partners' joint membership add £3 (for concessionary rates both members must be eligible for the membership rate). Life membership information is available on request.

If you join by Direct Debit you will receive three months' membership extra, free!

Title _____ Surname _____ Forename(s) _____

Address _____

_____

_____ Post Code _____

Date of Birth _____ E-mail address _____

Signature _____

Partner's details if required

Title _____ Surname _____ Forename(s) _____

Date of Birth _____ E-mail address _____

Please tick here ☐ if you would like to receive occasional e-mails from CAMRA
(at no point will your details be released to a third party).

Find out more about CAMRA at **www.camra.org.uk**   *Telephone* 01727 867201

DIRECT Debit

✂ detached and retained this section

CAMPAIGN FOR REAL ALE

Instruction to your Bank or Building Society to pay by Direct Debit

DIRECT Debit

Please fill in the form and send to: Campaign for Real Ale Ltd. 230 Hatfield Road, St. Albans, Herts. AL1 4LW

Name and full postal address of your Bank or Building Society

To The Manager _____ Bank or Building Society

Address _____

Postcode _____

Name (s) of Account Holder (s)

Bank or Building Society account number

Branch Sort Code

Reference Number

Banks and Building Societies may not accept Direct Debit Instructions for some types of account

Originator's Identification Number

9	2	6	1	2	9

FOR CAMRA OFFICIAL USE ONLY
This is not part of the instruction to your **Bank or Building Society**

Membership Number

Name

Postcode

Instruction to your Bank or Building Society

Please pay CAMRA Direct Debits from the account detailed on this Instruction subject to the safeguards assured by the Direct Debit Guarantee. I understand that this instruction may remain with CAMRA and, if so, will be passed electronically to my Bank/Building Society

Signature(s)

Date